Wizards of Media Oz

Behind the Curtain of Mainstream News

Norman Solomon

and

Jeff Cohen

Common Courage Press   Monroe, Maine

Library of Congress Cataloging-in-Publication Data
Solomon, Norman, 1951—
Wizards of media Oz:
behind the curtain of mainstream news/
Norman Solomon and Jeff Cohen.
p. cm.
Includes index.
ISBN 1-56751-118-X (paper : alk. paper)
ISBN 1-56751-119-8 (cloth : alk. paper)
1. Journalism--Objectivity. 2. Mass media--Objectivity.
3. Journalistic ethics. 4. Mass media--Moral and ethical aspects.
I. Cohen, Jeff, 1951- . II. Title.
PN4784.O24S66 1997
302.23--dc21   97-9691
CIP

Common Courage Press
Box 702
Monroe, ME 04951

207-525-0900   fax: 207-525-3068

First Printing

**This book is dedicated to
our beloved parents and in-laws**

Miriam & Morris Solomon
and
Millicent & James Higgins

Viola & Sol Cohen
and
Bertine & Earl Kristal

Contents

Part V
"Public Broadcasting" Tunes Out the Public

Part VI
Health in the Marketplace

Part VII
Affirmative Re-Action

Part VIII
Media Haves and Have-Nots

Part IX
Media Idols and Pariahs

Part X
The Reign of the "Dixiecan" Congress

Part XI
Campaign '96: Status vs. Quo

Part XII
Mediated History

Part XIII
When News Media Serve the CIA

Part XIV
Human Rights, Media Wrongs

Part XV
Media-Speak

Part XVI
Fun and Games and Prizes

Introduction

When I was young and easy, an old Wobbly rewarded me with a tattered copy of *The Brass Check* by Upton Sinclair. The title referred to the coin that young brothel women were handed by their tricks; they, in turn, cashed them in with their madam at the end of their day's labors.

Sinclair's game, however, was not the kept woman; it was the kept press. The former recognized her work as demeaning; the latter served their publishers, if not tremulously, gladly. And righteously. Need we mention William Randolph Hearst and his derring-do reporters covering—or, in the words of San Simeon's master, furnishing—the Spanish-American War?

A century later, our press, especially the Respectables, have gone Hearst one better. They helped make the Gulf War yellow ribbon time. It was glory, glory all the way. Our most prestigious journals found the horrors visited by our smart bombs upon Iraqi women and kids news not fit to print. It is no secret that our media—TV and radio, owned by the same Big Boys, compounding the obscenity—played the role of bat boys to the sluggers of the Pentagon.

A grotesque case in point: A young TV journalist, covering the bomb devastation to Iraqi civilian districts, was fired by the chief of NBC News. "Jon Alpert was a man with a cause and a mission," explained the chief. He was not objective.

My old friend, James Cameron, the nonpareil of British journalists, spoke with some authority in this matter. During the darkest days of the Vietnam War, he had visited Hanoi, the first Western journalist to do so. On coming to the United States, he brought forth the astonishing news that the North Vietnamese were humans, not unlike ourselves. He was as a matter of course excoriated in all our media, especially by the most respected and prestigious. "If not downright mischievous, I was certainly 'non-objective.'" He had committed the unpardonable sin of challenging official, and thus accepted, truths. "I have always tended to argue that objectivity was of less importance than the truth, and that the reporter, whose technique was informed by no opinion, lacked a very serious dimension."

Upton Sinclair was not "objective," he was merely seeking the truth. How come *The Brass Check*, as timely today as it was then, is not a best seller? What's good enough for Colin Powell should be good enough for Sinclair, even if posthumously so.

Fortunately for our sanity and self-respect, there have always been the muckrakers; those few who have challenged the official truth, who have obstinately sought out the hard truth.

In Sinclair's time, there were Lincoln Steffens and Ida Tarbell, among the contumacious trouble-makers. Further along came the indomitable George Seldes, his *Lords of the Press* and his wondrous newsletter, *In fact*, that kept us from living in total darkness. And, of course, the north star of independent journalists, I.F. Stone and his revelatory weekly.

Today we are blessed with a couple of young investigative journalists, Norman Solomon and Jeff Cohen, who along with their media watch colleagues at FAIR are letting in the light. In FAIR's magazine, *EXTRA!*, I am finding all the news that the Respectables find unfit to print. It is great therapy for me; it keeps my blood pressure down and my skull from going numb.

Now, Solomon and Cohen have gathered some of their columns into a lovely compendium, undressing the "liberal media." They call it *Wizards of Media Oz: Behind the Curtain of Mainstream News*. It is an eye-opener.

Don't leave home without it.

Studs Terkel

Part I
Behind the Curtain

At the end of the 20th century, we're off to see the wonderful wizardry of a multimedia future. But we may not realize that political leaders and media owners are far cozier than appearances usually indicate—while reporters and pundits are much more likely to stroke the corporate establishment than nip at its prestigious heels.

Tryst on a Love Boat:
Politicians and Media Magnates

For media tycoons and their favorite politicians, it was a love boat. For media consumers, it was a cruise to nowhere.

On the first day of summer [1995], mega-media owners and other corporate heavies boarded an old aircraft carrier on the Hudson River in New York City for a gala fundraising dinner—a "Salute to Newt Gingrich" that grossed $1.7 million for the Republican Congressional Committee's 1996 war chest.

Conveners of the dinner included News Corp. head Rupert Murdoch and Time Warner chairman Richard Parsons. The assembled media magnates had good reason to celebrate: Only a few days earlier, the U.S. Senate showered them with enough gifts to make Santa Claus look like Silas Marner.

In Washington-ese, the legislation is known as the "Telecommunications Competition and Deregulation Act." Consumer advocates call it the Time Warner Enrichment Act—but such critics are apt to get little media notice. (Funny thing about that.)

The giveaway sailed through the Senate on June 15 with bipartisan support, 81 to 18. But in the race to aid media conglomerates, Republican senators led the charge.

The Senate bill bestows many favors, such as:

- permitting a single company to own an almost unlimited number of radio stations;

- letting one corporation buy up as many TV stations as it wants until transmitting to 35 percent of the nation's population;

- freeing cable TV monopolies from price controls that have saved consumers over $3 billion since being enacted by Congress (over President Bush's veto) in 1992.

When the House passes its version of the bill later this summer, supporters will include about 80 House Republicans who flew from the nation's capital in a chartered plane and corporate jets to attend the floating fundraiser June 21.

Years from now, looking back on the summer of 1995, we may remember it as the season when the media giants broke free of nearly all public interest regulation and anti-trust constraints.

By the year 2000 or so, the bulk of the country's media outlets could be owned by a half-dozen firms. We tend to forget that just a few years ago, before anyone had ever heard of "Time Warner," there was a company named Time and another called Warner. Now, huge merged companies swallow up other huge merged companies. Would you believe Time Warner Turner Bell Atlantic TCI News Corp.?

As media critic A.J. Liebling put it a few decades ago, "Freedom of the press is guaranteed only to those who own one."

But these days, it's not just "the press" that's involved. From broadcast outlets and cable systems to satellites and computer technologies, fewer and fewer companies dominate as they keep getting bigger.

What's wrong with that? Ask a few journalists. Especially in private, they're likely to express misgivings—or outright anger—about the bottom-line mentality now determining newsroom priorities. If you're sick of so much "infotainment" coverage and so little news substance, you're not alone.

The Senate-approved bill would make the situation much worse. Yet, in theory at least, all is not lost. After both houses of Congress take final action, the bill will reach President Clinton's desk. He could veto it.

But a veto would require political courage. And Clinton, like most politicians in Washington, is a paper tiger who prefers to growl at media moguls in public while purring at their feet behind the scenes.

It's one thing to rail against violence and smut coming out of Hollywood and the music industry, as Sen. Bob Dole did last month when he publicly lambasted Time Warner. But, at the same time, Dole was the moving force behind the Senate bill providing multi-billion-dollar windfalls and unprecedented power for Time Warner.

That bill, points out Jeff Chester of the Washington-based Center for Media Education, "will increase the control that a handful of companies—including Time Warner—have over the media culture, and will make them less accountable to the public."

"The whole concept of local television, local broadcasting, is threatened by this bill," says TV critic Tom Shales, "because if some big...communications superpower can buy all these local television stations, there ain't gonna be local television stations anymore... [They are] just going to be prepackaged, freeze-dried...and every television station will look alike."

Sen. Bob Kerrey, the Nebraska Democrat who led opposition to the bill, is hardly an anti-corporate firebrand. But he couldn't stomach the legislation's extreme provisions. "Ultimately, this bill is about power," Kerrey noted. "The bottom line is that in this bill, corporations have it and consumers don't."

Warning of the increased media power that Congress seeks to place in the hands of a few, Rep. Edward Markey (D-Mass.) said: "It would make Citizen Kane look like an underachiever."

Under the banner of "deregulation," Time Warner and TCI — the two biggest cable companies in the country—would be able to drastically hike cable rates. Meanwhile, Time Warner and TCI could merge with phone companies, buy more broadcast stations and control both the content and delivery systems of TV programming.

So, it's no wonder that the head of Time Warner anteed up $100,000 as co-chairman of the recent GOP fundraising bash on a ship in the Hudson River. It may have been billed as a "Salute to Newt Gingrich," but when corporate media brass are on board, politicians seem to be the ones doing most of the saluting.

[Bill Clinton signed the Telecommunications Act in February 1996; months later, Time Warner's merger with Turner Broadcasting won federal approval, creating the biggest media/entertainment company in the world.]

June 28, 1995

The Distant Stars
of the Pundit Elite

Are you tired of TV politics shows? We're talking about the programs starring elite insiders—pundits who've grown so close to the money and power corrupting Washington that they're almost blind to the corruption.

Here's our proposal for a totally new TV show, with a panel of interesting, informed, down-to-earth people: perhaps a teacher, auto worker, nurse, retiree, small business owner and homemaker.

Instead of chatter among Washington's nobility, the show would feature people of ordinary means debating the issues and questioning those in power. It would be less like "Meet the Press" than "Meet the Oppressed." Less like "This Week With David Brinkley" than "This Week With Roseanne Conner"—the canny heroine of the TV sitcom.

And let's give our panel of workaday pundits—busy all week at their jobs—research help to allow them to fashion pointed questions on issues like taxes, trade, subsidies and campaign finance.

A strict rule would be needed: If any of our working-class pundits evolve into stars who accept $30,000 for a one-hour speech, they'll immediately be fired—and replaced by folks whose incomes are about $30,000 per *year*, close to the country's median family income.

Why is a new show necessary? Because the existing punditocracy has lost touch with most of us. They don't just inhabit a different neighborhood, but a different planet.

Let's pilot a spacecraft around the studio of ABC's *This Week With David Brinkley*.

GEORGE WILL: The well-connected Will insists that viewers have no right to know about his connections.

In April [1995], Brinkley's executive producer asked Will—before interviewing Bob Dole—to reveal that his wife would soon be communications director of the Dole presidential campaign. Will claims the disclosure was unnecessary, even though Dole's answers to Will's future questions will be partly shaped by Will's wife.

In recent weeks, Will has crusaded—on the Brinkley show and in his syndicated column—against Bill Clinton's sanctions on Japanese auto imports. When newspapers reported that Will's wife, Mari Maseng Will, was paid $199,000 in 1994 to lobby for the Japan Automobile Manufacturers Association, Will denied any duty to disclose that fact. "I was for free trade long before I met my wife," said Will.

On our proposed non-elite pundit show, an auto worker moonlighting as a pundit would probably offer a different perspective on how "free trade" affects the U.S. economy.

COKIE ROBERTS: Few would mistake Roberts for a working-class hero. Her dad and mom were both members of Congress. Her brother, Thomas Boggs, is a top corporate lobbyist. Her establishment views are imbued with an attitude that she was born into power and deserves to stay there.

The June [1995] issue of *American Journalism Review* shows that Roberts resents scrutiny of how she supplements her six-figure income from ABC-TV and National Public Radio. *AJR* says she received $35,000 two months ago to speak at a Junior League business conference in Fort Lauderdale—a fee supplied by JM Family Enterprises, a giant Toyota distributor.

According to the *Chicago Tribune*, Cokie and Steven Roberts, her TV-pundit husband, picked up $45,000 from a Chicago bank for a joint appearance in October [1994]. Now that's togetherness.

On Feb. 20 [1995], the couple was scheduled to speak at a gathering of Philip Morris executives, but Steve had to appear alone when Cokie canceled at the last moment. Philip Morris, the country's biggest cigarette manufacturer, is a force on Capitol Hill—the beat that Cokie Roberts covers.

On our "outside the beltway" show, it's likely that a nurse on the panel—having seen the effects of tobacco up close—would be less cozy with Philip Morris.

SAM DONALDSON: A multimillionaire who has pocketed up to $30,000 per speech to corporate gatherings, Donaldson holds down the "left wing" of the Brinkley show. He has also pocketed $97,000 in federal wool and mohair subsidies in the last two years for owning a ranch in New Mexico. He lives in a suburb of Washington, D.C.

On the people's pundit show, we'd probably hear a different perspective on agriculture from a family farmer struggling to earn in a year what Donaldson earns from one speech.

DAVID BRINKLEY: The show's host exudes an air of being above it all. But he's not above taking fees—$18,000 per speech —from Washington's special interests to entertain the executive class. Unlike most working-class people, Brinkley opposes increased taxes on the wealthiest Americans. He ridiculed such a proposal as a "sick stupid joke" in a 1992 speech to a trucking industry group.

Last July [1994], Brinkley joined Cokie Roberts, Sam Donaldson and other ABC News stars in formally protesting the network's hesitant limits on outside lecture fees.

Maybe a real-life Roseanne Conner—whose smart-alecky outlook doesn't stem from an elite perch on the world—would be an ideal host of a pundit show.

We believe many TV viewers are ready to watch this kind of "outside the beltway" show. But is there a TV network ready to air it? And sponsors ready to fund it?

As Roseanne would say, "Don't hold your breath."

[David Brinkley gave up his hosting role on *This Week* in November 1996.]

June 7, 1995

THERE'S SIMPLY NO DEBATE.

Number one in America for the past 14 years.

"... still the best of all political talk shows." - Tom Shales, *The Washington Post* December 24, 1995

THISWEEK
with *David Brinkley*

11:30 AM

Unwittingly candid headline in ad tells what's missing from *This Week*'s elite panel.

Public Loses
in Radio "Gold Rush"

What's happening to American radio right now is a crying shame—but few tears are being shed.

In the weeks since the landmark Telecommunications Act of 1996 became law, a frenzy of radio deals has sent profiteers laughing all the way to the bank. Meanwhile, the victims—the American people—remain clueless.

Except for stories on business pages, mainstream news outlets are saying little about the huge shakeup in the radio industry. Newspapers and magazines devote plenty of ink to television. And TV is fascinated with itself. But, overall, radio gets little media attention.

That's especially unfortunate these days—because the new law has opened the floodgates by lifting limits on how many radio stations a single firm can own. National curbs have been abolished, and local caps have been boosted so high that a big city can have eight radio stations owned by the same corporation.

One result: Infinity Broadcasting Corp. now owns 46 radio stations nationwide, including a dozen it bought for $410 million a couple of weeks ago [in March 1996].

Even before passage of the new law, media conglomerates sensed what was coming: 1995 saw "the largest group of radio transactions in the history of the world," says Scott Ginsburg, the gleeful head of the ever-bigger Evergreen Media Corp.

And we ain't seen nothin' yet. Since Feb. 8 [1996], when Bill Clinton signed the Telecommunications Act, radio mergers and buyouts have been worth an average of half-a-billion dollars each week.

The *Wall Street Journal* reports that "the telecommunications legislation has triggered a gold rush of the airwaves." A lot more than money is at stake. Those airwaves will be carrying whatever is most profitable—even if it's sleaze, hate-talk or misinformation.

Infinity Broadcasting, a dominant force in major radio markets, has just finalized a new five-year contract with its brightest syndicated star, the proudly crude Howard Stern. And now, Infinity plans to premiere "The Howard Stern Radio Network"— described by *Advertising Age* magazine as "24 hours of talk and music from jocks picked by Mr. Stern."

In the craven new world of mega-radio, it doesn't matter that Stern often denigrates women and racial minorities on the air. Commercial success qualifies him to judge who else should be promoted on national radio.

Infinity's other talk-radio hosts include G. Gordon Liddy, who has counseled listeners on the most effective ways to shoot federal law-enforcement agents. For a time, the company also syndicated Bob Grant, a spewer of racial hatred against immigrants, African-Americans and others.

Last month, when mammoth Jacor Communications Inc. paid $770 million to snap up 19 more radio outlets as well as a pair of TV stations, the firm's president, Randy Michaels, was ecstatic: "We think the opportunity of owning a gazillion radio stations and a television station in one market is terrific."

Lost in all the money-mad euphoria is the fact that the airwaves are supposed to belong to the public.

America's 10,200 commercial radio stations don't provide much diversity. With few exceptions, the "news" and "public affairs" range from inadequate to pitiful.

Even many "public" stations have become homogenized. Political reporter Cokie Roberts sounds about the same whether she's reporting for National Public Radio or the Disney-owned ABC network. Despite more lengthy coverage and a more erudite style, the gist of NPR News increasingly resembles what's on commercial networks.

Yet, radio still is enriching the lives of many listeners. Some independent-minded broadcasters are sticking to their mission.

Consider what one man named David Barsamian has accomplished. Ten years ago, with no money but lots of determination, working out of his home in Boulder, Colorado, he started a national program called *Alternative Radio*, featuring speeches by people rarely heard in mass media.

Today, *Alternative Radio* is a mainstay on more than 100 non-commercial radio stations, which receive the weekly hour-long program via satellite. The speakers are articulate, committed to progressive social change—and quite unlike what we usually hear on the radio.

In this high-tech era, radio retains the positive power to break through clichés that divide or confuse us. Unadorned, the sound of the human voice can resonate profoundly.

The wondrous potential of radio makes its current predicament all the more tragic.

[In June 1996, three months after this column was written, Westinghouse/CBS announced its acquisition of Infinity Broadcasting for $4.9 billion—creating, in the words of *Newsweek*, "the biggest radio company since people huddled around their sets listening to FDR."]

March 20, 1996

Part II
It Takes Class

The era of big government may be over, but the epoch of big money shows no sign of abating. While aspects of government are often subjected to media scrutiny, the prerogatives of business rarely undergo in-depth probing; this is quite helpful to wielders of private wealth.

When "Big" is Bad—
And When It Isn't

"Big government" has emerged as one of the most reviled villains of American political rhetoric. From Capitol Hill to the campaign trail—and in routine media discourse—the scourge of large government is self-evident and menacing.

In contrast, we rarely hear warnings about "big business." The fact that some giant companies keep expanding their size and power is accepted as beneficial at best, a mixed blessing at worst. The dangers of "big business" are apt to get short shrift.

Why the wide gap in perceptions?

For decades, news outlets have been hammering government: from city halls, county boards and state legislatures to Congress and the White House. Under the glare of media spotlights, government can look awful—with defects ranging from chronic inefficiency to notable corruption.

Small wonder that many Americans are convinced the public sector is dysfunctional and perhaps downright evil.

The private sector, however, generally eludes media scrutiny. Its activities are ordinarily assumed to require little accountability, much less approval, from the public.

Although they can affect our lives as much as government actions do, major decisions by big-asset firms are usually relegated to the financial press, or to the business sections of mainstream newspapers and magazines. Reporting tends to focus narrowly on prospects for corporate profits.

Ironically, while we keep hearing that bloated entitlements for health care and Social Security are out of control, the "big-government" tag is not applied to an agency that spends nearly three-quarters of a billion dollars each day. The Department of Defense seems to be immune from sustained media criticism for being too big or too expensive.

Not coincidentally, the Pentagon has been a cash-cow customer for many Fortune 500 companies. Some of them—such as

General Electric and Westinghouse—have huge investments in media. Lots more of them are high-spending advertisers, as well as moneyed contributors to politicians who selectively lambast "big government."

NBC Nightly News has presented a regular feature, "The Fleecing of America"—focusing, in the words of anchor Tom Brokaw, on "how your government is wasting your money." NBC (owned by GE) has not yet offered regular segments on "how corporate America is ripping you off."

Scandals in the private sector, like the S&L debacle, are often under-covered—as taxpayers and consumers lose billions. Meanwhile, broadcast and print media fixate on relatively petty government scandals like congressional check-bouncing.

Even news accounts of polls skew our attention in one direction. Polling questions commonly measure disapproval of government waste, graft and deception—but rarely touch on private-sector waste, fraud and abuse. For example, the private health-insurance industry is one of the biggest—and most costly—bureaucracies in our country.

Two years ago, the Associated Press conducted a poll with questions like, "What percent of the federal budget do you realistically think could be cut as wasteful?"

But we don't often hear similar queries to gauge public discontent with big business, such as: "Are corporate profits and CEO salaries excessive? What percentage do you think could be redirected toward employee wages, job training, safer working conditions or environmental protection?"

Reporters and editors *do* provide a valuable public service when they tenaciously dig behind facades of government virtue. Journalists should insist on ferreting out malfeasance among elected officials and their appointees.

However, it's much less common for newsrooms to encourage journalists to go after powerful corporations with similar zeal. The hazards are many.

Corporations can sue for libel. They can withdraw advertising—and perhaps encourage other companies to do the same. And large corporate entities are run by people who tend to hobnob with media owners.

"The First Amendment rights belong to the owners," says Nicholas Johnson, a former member of the Federal Communications Commission. "And the owners can exercise those rights by hiring people who will hire journalists who don't rock the boat, who don't attack advertisers, who don't challenge the establishment. That's a form of censorship."

In truth, few "successful" reporters make a habit of tough reporting on corporations. Yet, we live in a time when corporate policies have enormous effects on our lives—from the workplace and the marketplace to the economy and the environment.

As former *Washington Post* reporter Morton Mintz pointed out in Harvard's *Nieman Reports* a few years ago: "It is beyond doubt that the large corporation has always governed, most importantly by deciding whether untold numbers of people will live or die, will be injured, or will sicken."

He added: "For decades now, the corporate potential to inflict bodily harm has been increasing rapidly, by reason of the onward march of perilous new technologies—chemical, nuclear, and others."

For the most part, news media seem to be in denial about corporate power and its importance in our lives. That, according to Mintz, is a major journalistic flaw: "Underlying the pathetically inadequate coverage of life-threatening corporate misconduct is the everlasting embrace by the press of a truly absurd but wondrously convenient rationale for pro-corporate tilt: in an industrial society government constitutes the whole of governance."

With news coverage casting aspersions on government agencies while letting corporations slide, it's easy for many politicians to denounce "big government" while winking at big business.

October 11, 1995

When a Network TV Reporter Moonlights as a Lobbyist

Imagine that a prominent network TV correspondent regularly made partisan speeches on a major policy issue, accepted big lecture fees from groups on one side of the debate, and even went to Capitol Hill to speak in behalf of that position.

And imagine that the reporter's coverage of the issue was blatantly one-sided, while he openly boasted in press interviews that he saw his job as advancing that one side.

In such a case, the TV network—for credibility's sake — would surely reassign that correspondent to a different issue. Right?

Wrong—as long as the reporter espouses a cause dear enough to the heart of network management. That's the case with John Stossel, the ABC correspondent who crusades on and off the air against government regulation of business.

For years, Stossel has used his top reporting post at ABC's *20/20* to attack environmental regulations.

In a 1988 segment titled "Much Ado About Nothing?" Stossel was so eager to question bans on unsafe chemicals that he grossly understated the dangers of dioxin. In "The Town That Loves Garbage," he hailed landfills and pooh-poohed environmentalists who call for conservation.

His December 1992 segment extolling the virtues of food irradiation ignored medical specialists who question its safety. This allowed Stossel to make wild unrebutted claims, like: "Thirty countries have been irradiating food for years without problems." Unmentioned was the fact that nations like Austria, Germany, Sweden and Switzerland have banned food irradiation, and that the main countries using radiation to process food were China, the former Soviet Union and apartheid South Africa—not places known for free debate on environmental matters.

Besides his *20/20* work, Stossel now hosts hour-long ABC specials. In April [1994], the first one—"Are We Scaring Ourselves to Death?"—was a broadside against federal health and safety rules. "Scientists say many of our fears about chemicals are ridiculous," Stossel proclaimed. And: "Economists say regulation makes a country a little poorer."

Unknown to viewers, two of the three producers hired to work on Stossel's special had resigned—because their research, including data that showed product safety regulation to be cost-effective, did not conform to Stossel's preconceived beliefs.

But who needs facts when you've got an ideology—and a powerful network ready to back you?

It's apparent that ABC/Capital Cities management shares Stossel's opposition to federal regulation of business (though it likes federal subsidies). On Jan. 19 [1995], ABC's Thomas Murphy— along with Rupert Murdoch, Ted Turner and several dozen CEOs from the country's biggest communications firms— held an unprecedented, closed-door conference with Republicans on Capitol Hill to discuss deregulating their industry. Consumer groups were excluded.

ABC backed Stossel after he gave a speech last November [1994] to the American Industrial Health Council—a group that includes Du Pont, Procter & Gamble, Pfizer and Squibb—telling the firms what they wanted to hear: Agencies like the Food and Drug Administration and the Environmental Protection Agency should be abolished. "They don't make life safer. They make life less safe...because they interfere with the market." The Council paid Stossel $11,000 for the speech.

In recent months, Stossel has lectured to other pro-corporate pressure groups, including the Cato Institute, the Heartland Institute, the Chemical Council of New Jersey and the American Council on Capital Formation.

On Jan. 17 [1995], the reporter-activist turned quasi-lobbyist when he addressed members of Congress who've formed a new deregulation caucus. Stossel declared that regulation "in most cases does more harm than good.... The market polices itself."

Stossel later said it would have been wrong to go to Congress to "lobby for some specific bill, but I'm delighted to pitch the miracle of markets and the evils of regulation every chance I get."

Here's a reporter who takes money from (and shares podiums with) political interests on one side of the corporate regulation debate—then takes their message to Congress.

ABC might defend Stossel on the grounds that he keeps his off-screen ideology and activism separate from his on-air reporting—but such a defense is refuted by Stossel himself. Promoting his latest special in October [1994], an attack on various federal programs, he told a reporter: "I have come to believe that markets are magical and are the best protectors of the consumer. It is my job to explain the beauties of the free market."

January 25, 1995

Kathie Lee,
Disney
and Their Sweatshops

Controversy about Kathie Lee Gifford's clothing line has thrown harsh light on a TV star accused of profiting from labor at sweatshops. While Gifford took the heat, the conglomerate that owns her show—the Walt Disney Co.—appeared cool and above the fray. But that's not fair.

Disquieting facts about Gifford's commercial ventures have surfaced recently. Some of the clothes with her name on the label came from a Honduran factory with girls as young as 12 working in abysmal conditions. Other Kathie Lee garments hail from a Manhattan sweatshop where even the paltry wages for adults went unpaid.

These revelations are painful for Gifford, who co-hosts the *Live With Regis & Kathie Lee* program. Meanwhile, in private, Disney executives worry that news media might get around to widening the story. Their nightmare echoes the famous Mouseketeer tune ("Who's the leader of the club...") with a present-day version: "Who's the firm with sweatshops that make clothes for you and me? D-I-S...N-E-Y..."

In Haiti, poor women produce Disney clothing such as Pocahontas T-shirts and Lion King outfits for kids. Charles Kernaghan—the labor-rights activist whose congressional testimony blew the whistle on the Kathie Lee factory in Honduras—says that Disney relies on exploited Haitian labor.

"The wages are so low that the indentured workers live from debt to debt in utter misery," Kernaghan told us. The setup in Haiti is hardly fly-by-night, he added. Disney has been buying clothes from the same contractor for 20 years.

In May [1996], while Disney continued to escape media scrutiny of its own consumer products, the company did what it could to stabilize Kathie Lee Gifford's career. When she failed to shake off the scandal, Disney wheeled out a big gun: ABC News.

In a hastily arranged May 22 segment, ABC's *PrimeTime Live* tried to bolster a sagging reputation. After Diane Sawyer acknowledged that Gifford's syndicated show and ABC are both owned by Disney, *PrimeTime* proceeded with sympathetic—even fawning—treatment.

The suffering of sweatshop employees got short shrift. Instead, the focus was on the anguish of Gifford, who exuded tearful innocence: "I felt like I was being—of all people, being kicked in the teeth for—for trying to help kids." The program touted Gifford's good works for charities.

However, the next day brought a jolting PR setback. News broke that—just a few blocks from her TV studio in New York City—a sweatshop was turning out Kathie Lee blouses for Wal-Mart. Hired to work below minimum wage for up to 60 hours a week, many of the employees hadn't been paid.

The entrepreneur's husband, ABC sportscaster Frank Gifford, responded by rushing to the sweatshop with envelopes of $300 in cash for the mistreated workers. The incident dramatized a blindspot that the Giffords share with many journalists: placing emphasis on the momentary balm of charity rather than the long-term solution of justice.

Even now, Kathie Lee Gifford doesn't seem to grasp the extent of the problem. In a statement that her publicist faxed to us on May 28, Gifford claimed that "there are a handful of unethical manufacturers."

But it's not a matter of a "handful." Thousands of deplorable garment factories operate in the United States. "There are about 22,000 cutting and sewing shops, and about half of them are really sweatshops," according to Labor Secretary Robert Reich.

Under pressure from labor-rights activists, Kathie Lee Gifford has announced an inspection program for all factories producing her line of clothes. The rigor of the process remains to be seen. But at least Gifford has acknowledged a problem—which is more than can be said for the Walt Disney Co.

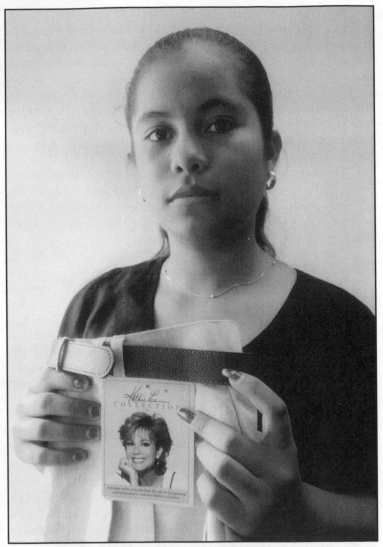

Wendy Diaz, 15, one of Kathie Lee's child laborers in Honduras

So far, Disney has managed to stay clear of media brickbats over sweatshops. Such avoidance is easier when a company owns many large media outlets.

Disney casts a giant media shadow since its purchase of ABC last year. The firm's broadcast and cable networks combine with divisions that handle TV syndication, book publishing, high-tech multimedia and, of course, movies.

But all of Disney's media glitz means nothing to impoverished women who work for pennies an hour.

May 29, 1996

The Great Disappearing Issue
of 1996

Months ago, it was *the* political issue. Today, corporate greed isn't even on the mass media's radar screen.

For a short while, news outlets were doing a lot of big stories about "downsizing"—the widespread firing of workers by companies eager to boost profits. But soon, most of the press simply dropped the subject.

That was easy to do after Patrick Buchanan's 1996 presidential campaign collapsed in early spring. For Wall Street interests, Buchanan served as an ideal adversary. With a media-hyped enemy like him, CEOs making seven figures didn't need too many friends.

Running in the Republican primaries, Buchanan emerged as an anti-corporate crusader with a pitchforked tongue, shouting "Lock and load!" His assorted bigotries—toward people failing to be white, Christian and heterosexual—helped sink his campaign. Along the way, Buchanan rebuked corporations with a message so garbled that he didn't even support the basic union rights of American workers.

Since then, maltreatment of workers has virtually disappeared as an issue in the '96 campaign. While Bill Clinton and Bob Dole differ on details of economic policy, they are both firmly in the pockets of the downsizers.

Their only opponent with a chance to finish in double digits, Ross Perot, does question the anti-democratic provisions in "free trade" pacts. But he has earned such a reputation for wackiness that the pseudo-populist billionaire hardly worries corporate defenders.

The only person running for president who could demolish the Republicrat doubletalk about corporations is Ralph Nader. The long-time consumer advocate will be on the ballot in about half the states. But don't look for Nader at the presidential debates this fall; Clinton strategists are sure to block him.

The media role in all this is discouraging. The national press corps doesn't seem very interested in a topic unless a "major" candidate is talking about it. So, the issue of corporate power is off the media map.

"Too much of the coverage treats downsizing and other economic problems as though they were just like natural disasters," says Scott Nova, director of a new research outfit based in Washington, D.C., the Preamble Center for Public Policy. "The reality is that downsizing, wage stagnation and the flow of American jobs overseas are products of specific decisions by corporations and government policy makers. And those decisions can be reversed—if we have the political will to do so."

Few of the nation's power brokers express alarm that international bodies such as the World Trade Organization can now override national standards on the environment, health protection and labor rights. "Policy elites in both parties are embracing a corporate global vision," Nova told us. And that vision is popular among the most influential reporters and pundits.

But Nova points to "a wide split between public opinion and elite opinion." Outside of corporate-government hierarchies, people are much less likely to be complacent about the status quo. And they're much more likely to want the government to restrict corporations.

According to a new poll, commissioned by the Preamble Center, 69 percent of registered voters "favor government action to promote more responsible corporate behavior and penalize bad corporate behavior." Fifty-four percent view downsizing as a problem "serious enough to warrant direct government intervention." And far more people blamed stagnating middle-class incomes on "corporate greed" (46 percent) than on "wasteful and inefficient government" (28 percent).

Even at its height last spring, media coverage of corporate greed tended to avoid discussion of specific remedies involving government action. But Americans in general appear to be quite open to such scenarios. "The public is still angry at government," comments pollster Ethel Klein, "but they are so fed up with—and frightened by—the way corporations are treating employees that they're willing to take a chance on government action."

Another researcher for the nationwide poll, Guy Molyneux, sees a shift in political ground: "With Americans increasingly recognizing corporate behavior as a central economic problem, political leaders are going to feel pressed to demonstrate their concern for average working people by demanding accountability from large corporations."

We may not hear much about it between now and Election Day, but the absence of corporate accountability is bound to return to center stage as a key issue in American politics.

September 4, 1996

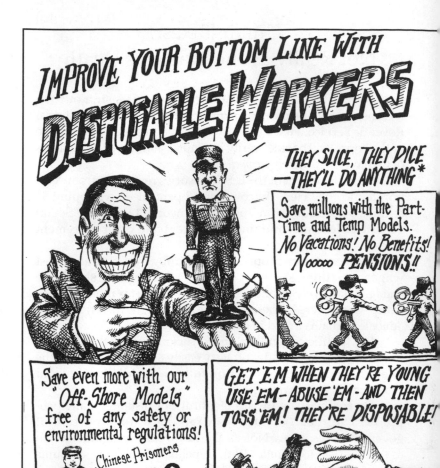

Unfair Taxes:
Not Really as Inevitable as Death

WASHINGTON—By the time most of us sign our tax returns, we're in no mood to stare at pie charts from the Internal Revenue Service. That's too bad, since diagrams on a back page of the Form 1040 booklet verify an impression shared by millions of taxpayers: *We're being ripped off.*

Only 10 percent of the U.S. Treasury's revenue is from "corporate income taxes." In contrast, 68 percent—a whopping $1 trillion—pours in from "personal income taxes" or "Social Security, Medicare, and unemployment and other retirement taxes."

With corporate profits soaring through the roof and most wages remaining stagnant or worse, this country should be engaged in a lively public debate about where tax money comes from—and where it goes. For the most part, however, national "debate"remains mired in evasive rhetoric.

Few politicians in Washington acknowledge that big corporations and the rich get off very easily at tax time—while the overwhelming bulk of taxation falls on middle-income and working-class Americans.

Diversionary myths are plentiful. For instance, many people believe that "welfare" is draining a huge portion of government resources. Not so. The key welfare program known as AFDC—Aid to Families With Dependent Children—accounts for just 1 percent of the federal budget.

In fact, the IRS reports, if you add up all the U.S. government spends on AFDC, Medicaid and food stamps plus "supplemental security income and related programs," you'll get a grand total of 12 percent of the federal budget. Another 6 percent is devoted to "health research and public health programs, unemployment compensation, assisted housing and social services."

Meanwhile, military spending soaks up 19 percent of federal outlays, not counting veterans benefits. In other words, about $5 billion is going to the Pentagon each week. For firms with military contracts, the Defense Department is a gigantic cash dispenser.

In the Nation's Capital, of course, preeminent movers and shakers don't ask basic questions about how the nation's capital gets distributed. Yet, outside the media spotlight, a significant congressional minority is thinking creatively.

Fifty-one members of the House belong to a group called the Progressive Caucus. In March [1996], they announced "an alternative framework for achieving a balanced federal budget in the next seven years." The scenario involves slashing "corporate welfare"—aid to dependent companies that costs taxpayers about $125 billion every year—about one-twelfth of the federal budget.

Chaired by Vermont's independent Rep. Bernie Sanders, the Progressive Caucus poses a feisty challenge to big-money tools on the Hill. Caucus members don't hem and haw about tax inequities. They get to the point.

Corporations "have seen their share of the nation's tax burden reduced from 32 percent in 1952 to 9 percent in 1992," Georgia Rep. Cynthia McKinney said last month. Another dissident Democrat, Rep. Peter DeFazio of Oregon, noted that "wasteful Pentagon spending" amounts to "the largest discretionary spending category in the entire federal budget."

If lawmakers agreed to make the tax code fairer and beat some modern-day swords into plowshares, the Progressive Caucus contends, the federal government could boost funding for vital efforts like "jobs programs, student loans, Head Start, environmental protection, crime prevention and affordable housing."

Numerous polls—including a recent nationwide survey by the Program on International Policy Attitudes at the University of Maryland—show that most Americans favor such shifts in spending priorities. However, proposals along those lines have been dead on arrival in Washington.

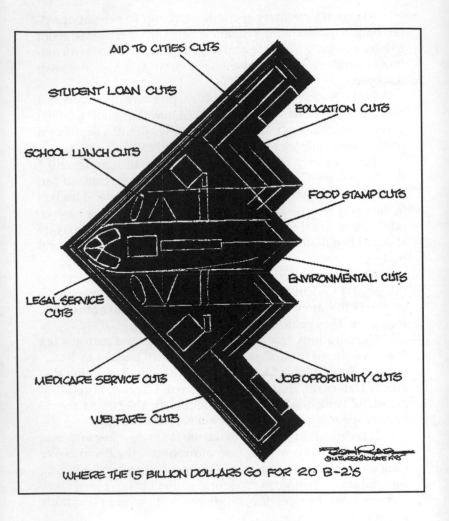

AID TO CITIES CUTS

STUDENT LOAN CUTS

EDUCATION CUTS

SCHOOL LUNCH CUTS

FOOD STAMP CUTS

ENVIRONMENTAL CUTS

LEGAL SERVICE CUTS

MEDICARE SERVICE CUTS

JOB OPPORTUNITY CUTS

WELFARE CUTS

WHERE THE 15 BILLION DOLLARS GO FOR 20 B-2'S

"The right wing has succeeded in redefining the terms of the federal budget debate so that even being a 'centrist' means supporting a budget balanced on the backs of the poor, the middle class and just about everyone except the wealthy and the Pentagon," says Bruce Allen of the Center for Economic Conversion.

Based in California's Silicon Valley, the center describes rival budget plans of the White House and the GOP as "dumb and dumber, respectively." Both entail major cuts in Medicare, Medicaid, AFDC and other social programs—but give more funds to the Pentagon.

This bleak situation doesn't have to go on forever. A system of equitable taxes and people-first spending is possible.

The saying goes that only two things are certain, death and taxes. Yet taxes need not be lamentable.

April 10, 1996

Part III
The Myth
of the Liberal Media

Millions of Americans believe in the existence of "the liberal media"—a notion peddled daily by many of the media's most powerful voices. The fact that few Americans ever hear a progressive critique of the mass media's conservative, pro-corporate tilt speaks volumes about the media's real biases.

TV Rightist Off and Running, Leftists Off the Screen

When Patrick Buchanan announced that he is taking a leave from TV punditry to prepare his campaign for president, the right-wing commentator did so on CNN's *Crossfire*—a show he has long co-hosted.

Buchanan's on-air announcement Feb. 16 [1995] was assisted by the supposedly leftist co-host of *Crossfire*, Michael Kinsley, who helped Buchanan hold up a sign giving his campaign's 800-number.

It was a telling moment—with Buchanan's 800-number displayed on the screen—symbolizing the submissive role that TV's lukewarm liberals play alongside TV's fiery rightists.

Consider what happened back on Dec. 16, 1991: *Crossfire* refused to let presidential candidate Jerry Brown appear as a guest when he insisted on the right to give out his campaign's 800-number. In Brown's absence, all four *Crossfire* pundits from right to "left" ridiculed the candidate as if he were a clown.

Kinsley asked: "Isn't Jerry Brown making a complete joke of himself, carrying on like this?"

If Pat Buchanan's campaign is a joke, the joke is on the media. He has used his status as a TV talking head and syndicated columnist to become a leading advocate of America's right-wing movements and causes. He is Mr. Anti—anti-tax, anti-gun control, anti-gay, anti-choice, anti-U.N., etc.—a movement conservative who often appears at rightist rallies.

Now he hopes to capitalize on his media visibility in a second run for the presidency.

Buchanan isn't the only conservative partisan who could convert a commentator's roost into future bids for political office. Rush Limbaugh is constantly asked to run for president. Conservative Linda Chavez, one of the leading female pundits on PBS and CNN, has already run for the Senate.

Everyone knows where conservative pundits stand on the issues—and, as a result, right-wing activists for various causes stand ready to enlist in their campaigns.

But try to imagine a left-wing pundit using the same TV springboard into electoral politics that Buchanan has used. You'll need a good imagination—because national television doesn't feature such persons.

On TV, those who are paired against rightists like Buchanan and George Will are definitely *not* movement progressives; they are people like Kinsley, Jack Germond, Mark Shields, Al Hunt, Sam Donaldson.

If we found these guys speaking at a rally for a progressive cause—whether it be single-payer health care or labor-law reform, affirmative action or rainforest preservation, abortion rights or gay rights—we'd faint. So would they.

Many who face off against the opinion brigade of the right are employed as "objective" journalists. CNN pitted Al Hunt against hardcore rightists while Hunt was the *Wall Street Journal*'s Washington bureau chief. ABC began pairing Sam Donaldson against columnist George Will while Donaldson was the network's White House correspondent.

Unlike their rightist counterparts, TV's "leftists" rarely take clear stands on the issues. Indeed, they can be adept wafflers, far more comfortable straddling the center than supporting the left. Unlike the rightists, they do not promote an agenda for dramatic change and do not proselytize for causes.

Not surprisingly, TV's "leftists" often come across as defenders of the status quo.

In a period when much of the public is anxious—even angry— about the current state of affairs, defending the status quo is an easy way to lose a debate.

Progressive movements—such as consumer rights, labor, feminism, ecology and civil rights—have millions of supporters, many of them active Democrats. They also have proposals to dramatically change the status quo. But they don't have network TV pundits who champion their causes day after day.

Imagine what would happen if Buchanan's "left" counterpart on CNN, Michael Kinsley, decided to make a run for elective office. He's been on TV almost every weekday since 1989. Would there be a ground swell of support from grassroots Democratic activists so important in primaries? More likely there'd be a ground swell of laughter—or indifference.

Progressives might remember Kinsley's column in *Time* magazine, "Thatcher for President," that praised Britain's right-wing prime minister. Black activists might recall Kinsley's tepid stand on affirmative action, and his commentaries on South Africa that seemed more sympathetic to F.W. De Klerk than to Nelson Mandela.

Consumer activists might recollect that when Dan Quayle proposed limiting civil suits—a business-backed measure—Kinsley pretty much endorsed it. Environmental and feminist leaders are also on record complaining that Kinsley does not adequately represent them.

In fairness to Kinsley, he is a talented writer and clever commentator. What he's *not* is an advocate for the American left.

Nor are the others who routinely debate the right wing on national television. Their motto could be: "I'm not a leftist, but I play one on television."

A single word may explain why bona fide progressives do not appear as regular TV pundits while conservatives are ubiquitous: *censorship.*

If you think there's a different explanation, try to get one from network executives. We've tried for years without success.

February 22, 1995

I'm not a leftist, but I play one on TV.

When Al Hunt of the Wall Street Journal represents the left on national television, you know something is seriously skewed. The same goes for Michael Kinsley, who weighs in nightly "from the left" on CNN Crossfire. And then there's Mark Shields on CNN and PBS.

It's a racket: TV public affairs programs routinely serve up narrow "debates" pitting rabid right-wingers against mushy moderates who purportedly speak for "the left." Hunt, Kinsley, Shields, ABC's Sam Donaldson... they're part of the hot-air brigade of mostly white male pundits who are so immersed in the system, and so cozy with the political and corporate interests controlling it, that they rarely offend the powers that be.

Yet they're on TV appearing as leftists, even though none of them are forceful advocates for the broad social movements—feminism, civil rights, labor, ecology, consumer rights, etc.—that constitute the American le...

Consumer Fraud

With progressives ... of
passes for new...
no...

projects in the United States." That's how Barbara Ehrenreich described FAIR, the media watch group that recently grabbed headlines when we released our report on "Rush Limbaugh's Reign of Error" in *EXTRA!*

Subscribe to *EXTRA!*, and month after month you'll receive a lively, provocative roundup of what's fair and what's flawed with today's news reporting. An antidote to disinformation overload, *EXTRA!* pinpoint... bias, inaccuracies and censorship in a concise... well-documented and cheeky forma...

FREE to Reade...

Subscr...
receive...
...

On Television, Political Talk
Flies with One Wing

Nobody would try to fly a plane with a right wing and no left wing.

But on national television, political discussion shows have just such an imbalance. No wonder those programs wobble so weirdly.

Take ABC's *This Week With David Brinkley*. Its pundit roundtable usually features rightist George Will along with establishment centrists Sam Donaldson and Cokie Roberts. No leftist need apply.

Now that ABC has hired conservative William Kristol as an on-air political analyst, the Brinkley show—whose executive producer is former Bush administration official Dorrance Smith —tilts even further rightward. A recent *This Week* roundtable was made up of Kristol, Will and Roberts.

Why add Kristol to the panel? Why offer two rightists and no leftists?

Or should we pretend Cokie Roberts is a firebrand of the left? In the real world, she might sue for slander if you called her "leftwing." The main "cause" she champions in Washington is the right of pundits to rake in big lecture fees from corporate interests.

But in the make-believe world of TV, Roberts is the kind of pro-corporate centrist who passes as a liberal, the only alternative offered to the fire-breathers of the right.

Network news executives and corporate sponsors seem to prefer TV debates that exclude half the political spectrum—the half led by advocates for middle-class consumers, labor, the environment, minorities and others critical of the status quo.

Right now, CNN's *Crossfire* is looking for a new co-host "on the left" to take on conservatives like Robert Novak and John Sununu. That role has been played by the departing Michael Kinsley, a columnist and self-described moderate.

Crossfire is the show that made a national TV star (and presidential candidate) out of its right-wing co-host, Patrick Buchanan.

But the man who originally co-hosted the show "from the left" is now little more than a trivia question: Tom Braden.

Braden had unique credentials for representing the left on CNN. He'd been a high-ranking CIA official in Western Europe involved in covert operations against the left. (LSD guru Timothy Leary made one of his more sober observations when he referred to *Crossfire* as "the left wing of the CIA debating the right wing of the CIA.")

Crossfire is now one of CNN's most watched shows, but it appears destined to remain as imbalanced as a one-winged airplane. The *Los Angeles Times* reported in late November [1995] that two "strong candidates" contending for Kinsley's job are Bob Beckel and Juan Williams, two men who frequently substitute for Kinsley and who alternate as co-hosts of *Crossfire Sunday*.

Formerly a Democratic campaign operative, Beckel now heads a lobbying and consulting firm that represents corporate clients like the Walt Disney conglomerate, long-distance phone companies and insurance firms involved in the battle over toxic waste cleanup.

As a pundit, Beckel's views are often quite conservative. He frequently advises the Democratic Party to move rightward. In 1993, he hailed President Clinton's effort to downsize government as a great tactic to force a "showdown" with liberal Democrats, relishing that "the unions will grumble, the left will scream..."

Beckel didn't just support the Gulf War; he denounced protesters as "punks." Last year, he applauded Clinton for rebuffing liberals who urged greater cuts in Pentagon spending.

With such views, is Beckel an appropriate voice to represent "the left"? In the real world, no. On TV, perfect.

The same could be said of Juan Williams, a *Washington Post* reporter. Search Williams' writings for his judgments on "liberals" or "the left," and you'll find more criticism than praise.

Williams starred in a historic *Crossfire* episode about the Clarence Thomas/Anita Hill clash. Substituting as the left co-host, Williams was supposed to be a counterweight to Pat Buchanan,

who wailed that liberal conspirators were persecuting Judge Thomas. But Williams agreed with Buchanan.

Two days later, it looked like Buchanan had written Williams' column attacking "so-called champions of fairness: liberal politicians, unions, civil rights groups and women's organizations." The column concluded that "liberals have become monsters"; it led conservative Sen. Orrin Hatch to repeatedly praise Williams as "a great journalist" at the Thomas hearings.

I'm Juan Williams, from the left. Real world, no. On TV, yes.

Williams, Beckel and other TV "leftists" often express support for the right wing of the Democratic Party. They are well-cast only because TV debates are pseudo-symmetrical—pitting conservative Republican pundits against conservative Democratic ones.

What if the political shoe were on the other foot? Imagine the protests from groups like the Christian Coalition if CNN debates regularly featured left-wing Democrats against pundits reflecting the centrist Republican views of Senators John Chafee, William Cohen or Mark Hatfield.

In recent weeks, the center-to-right TV pundit brigade has been expending surpluses of hot air about the budget. But we rarely hear calls for cuts in military spending. Or increased taxes on the wealthy. Or raising corporate income taxes—which accounted for 25 percent of federal expenditures in the 1960s but only about half that percentage now.

Outside of Washington TV studios—in the real world of grassroots politics, union halls, churches and college campuses—such proposals make sense to a lot of people.

In the real world, of course, airplanes with just one wing don't fly.

[To replace Kinsley, CNN ended up hiring centrist Democrat Geraldine Ferraro and California Democratic Party chair Bill Press. After this column was finished, CNN invited Jeff Cohen to test briefly for the job.]

November 29, 1995

The Rightward Slant
of America's Op-Ed Pages

[The following is adapted from a speech by Norman Solomon to the national Association of Opinion Page Editors annual convention in Atlanta on Nov. 3, 1995.]

I'm glad that we're crossing paths in this impressive building complex here at CNN Center before it becomes known as Time Warner Center.

My last visit to a CNN studio was a number of years ago, when I was a guest on *Crossfire*, paired with a very conservative Hollywood scriptwriter who was on the satellite screen from Los Angeles. A guy sitting next to me in the studio says, "From the right, I'm Patrick Buchanan"—and I could believe that. And then the other guy sitting next to me says, "From the left, I'm Tom Braden." And I'm thinking: This is Tom Braden, the former CIA official who once wrote an article for the *Saturday Evening Post* titled, "Why I'm Glad the CIA Is Immoral." This is supposed to be my tag-team partner.

Here's what I want to stress: Populism, historically and in the present day, has taken two general paths. Only one of them is well represented on TV, talk radio and even most op-ed pages.

The scapegoating road is well-traveled by the Buchanans and the Robert Novaks, the Rush Limbaughs and the G. Gordon Liddys. But those who have taken the other fork in a populist journey—progressives—are very sparsely represented.

It's true that op-ed pages do better than TV networks in terms of diversity. But that's a high jump over low standards.

Think of the names of the most widely syndicated liberal columnists and try to append the adjective "populist" to them —Anthony Lewis, Mary McGrory, Richard Cohen... In most cases it would be absurd.

Working as a syndicated columnist, I've been told by some op-ed editors: "We've got progressive views covered—we run

Anthony Lewis." This is the Anthony Lewis who wrote a column a couple of years ago denouncing labor unions for having the nerve to lobby against NAFTA… In fact, many of the most widely touted "liberal" columnists wouldn't know a working person if their limousine ran one over.

Overall, mass media offer the public either mainstream pundits who differ on how to shore up the status quo, or populists of the right-wing variety. Largely excluded are advocates of progressive populism who explicitly reject scapegoating and who challenge the power of large corporations.

Data provided by syndicates are not particularly reliable when we try to gauge exact numbers. But the most recent independent survey I'm aware of—by the Featurank organization back in 1990—found seven syndicated op-ed columnists who were each carried in more than 100 papers with combined circulation of over 10 million: George Will, James J. Kilpatrick, David Broder, Ellen Goodman, Mike Royko, William Safire and William F. Buckley.

The media's narrow range of discourse, from the near left to the far right, gives the public the impression that there are basically two positions worthy of debate—a continuum of support for corporate assumptions or a xenophobic, women-bashing, anti-gay, racialist "populism."

Why is the field of populist punditry ceded almost entirely to rightists? Put another way: Why is it so uncommon for media forums to include unabashedly progressive critiques of the negative effects of entrenched economic power?

Why can't we do a better job of broadening the range beyond Anthony Lewis to George Will—or, these days, Anthony Lewis to an extreme rightist like Joseph Sobran? When the boundaries have been widened in recent years, the expansion has almost invariably been rightward. This fall, a large newspaper [the *Philadelphia Inquirer*] began running Sobran's syndicated column with the explanation that it wanted to publish "unvarnished conservatism." But the same paper does not come close to publishing an "unvarnished" progressive column on any kind of a regular basis.

Here's an assessment that came from the editor of the Heritage Foundation's *Policy Review* journal, Adam Meyerson, in the late 1980s: "Journalism today is very different from what it was 10 or 20 years ago. Today, op-ed pages are dominated by conservatives. We have a tremendous amount of conservative opinion, but this creates a problem for those who are interested in a career in journalism after college.... If Bill Buckley were to come out of Yale today, nobody would pay much attention to him. He would not be that unusual...because there are probably hundreds of people with those ideas [and] they have already got syndicated columns."

The circumstances are not very different now. In recent years we've seen more gender, racial and ethnic diversity on editorial pages. That's a positive trend. But diversity of race and gender hardly guarantees diversity of ideas.

This summer [1995], the president of the New York Times Syndicate, John Brewer, told the National Society of Newspaper Columnists: "There are very few competitive markets left and fewer newspapers." But he added that space is still opening up for "certain kinds of features"—for instance, "conservative columns by minorities or women."

The media tilt means a very uphill battle for progressive columnists. And there's another factor that I want to mention. Reinforcing prevalent concepts, attitudes and ideas actually requires *less* time and space—it's like pressing pre-installed buttons. These are notions that are virtual keystrokes on the word processor of a John Leo or George Will or dozens of other syndicated columnists as they make their standard denunciations: political correctness, multiculturalism, counterculture, dependency, reverse discrimination...

But if you're really outside the range of conventional wisdoms, you need to build and explore themes that *aren't* in the mass-media air. That's all the more reason that progressives should have a regular place at the op-ed table, not just an occasional temporary seat.

Today, many lives are in the balance. The immense poverty in this country, let alone elsewhere in the world, is heart-breaking.

The Gingriches and the Clintons offer no plausible scenarios for substantially improving the situation. Their deference to corporate power precludes even considering serious remedies.

Meanwhile, the onward march of op-ed punditry reminds me of a scene in Mark Twain's book *Roughing It*: A group of hikers are wandering through snowy mountains; it's near dusk, the cold night is descending, and they're lost. Actually, they're feeling a bit frightened. So they're relieved to look ahead and see a trail of footprints. The trail seems sure to lead them to the safety of town. They follow the footsteps in the snow. But, oddly, shelter doesn't come into view. Instead, the men just keep walking—and they begin to notice that the trail of footprints is getting wider and wider. Finally, the awful truth begins to dawn on them: They've been following their own circular tracks.

Guns, Ammo, Hate
and Talk Radio

It's no secret that talk radio has long been dominated by conservative hosts—even in liberal cities. But most Americans are unaware of frightening new trends in radio talk shows.

Ask members of the public to describe the right edge of talk radio, and they're likely to mention Rush Limbaugh. Not even close. The spectrum has moved so far rightward that in many markets Limbaugh sounds like a moderate.

The shift is not just to the far right, but the armed right—with open conversation about doing away with "traitors."

And major media companies are behind some of the extremists.

Meet Chuck Baker, who follows Limbaugh for three hours on KVOR Radio in Colorado Springs. While Limbaugh speaks to the conservative movement, Baker speaks to the "patriot" movement about forming guerrilla squadrons and taking out the "slimeballs" in Congress.

"Patriots" rail against Bill Clinton and the plot toward global government known as the "New World Order"; they see gun control as a Big Brother conspiracy.

In Colorado, Baker has used his show to promote patriot militia groups. For months, he accompanied his rants against the government by mimicking the sound of a firing pin: "kching, kching." Attacking Sen. Howard Metzenbaum over the Brady (gun control) Bill, he said that you wouldn't be rid of the senator until you could stand over his grave, "put the dirt on top of the box and say, 'I'm pretty sure he's in there.'"

Baker has regularly interviewed leaders of the armed right, including Rev. Pete Peters, an anti-Semite who says that God wants gays dead and pontificates against race-mixing with minorities.

Last August [1994], Linda Thompson of the "Unorganized Militia of the United States" came on Baker's show to advocate an armed march on Washington to remove the "traitors" in Congress: "We have 2 million U.S. troops, half of them are out of the country.... All of the troops they could muster would be 500,000 people. They would be outnumbered five to one, if only 1 percent of the country went up against them."

Baker, broadcasting from a gun shop, responded positively—telling his guest that soldiers "would come over to our side."

A week later, a caller urged the formation of "an orchestrated militia," saying: "The problem we have right now is who do we shoot. Other than Kennedy, Foley and Mitchell, the others are borderline traitors. They're the kingpins right now, besides the Slick One [Clinton].... You've got to get your ammo."

Baker's response was sympathetic: "Am I advocating the overthrow of this government?.... I'm advocating the cleansing." Citing the power of the "masses in rebellion," he asked: "Why are we sitting here?"

Later that day, a caller accused Baker of advocating "armed rebellion." The talk host corrected her: "An armed revolution."

Weeks later, in October, a Baker listener—Francisco Martin Duran—fired nearly 30 bullets at the White House. Nearby, Duran's abandoned pickup sported a bumper sticker: "Fire Butch Reno"—a favorite Baker nickname for Attorney General Janet Reno.

Duran and scores of other listeners inspired by Baker had called a local congressional office in August to oppose a ban on assault weapons. So many calls were irate or obscene that Duran's threat to "go to Washington and take someone out" went unnoticed.

As a talk show host, Baker accepts no responsibility: "If he [Duran] thinks I and Rush Limbaugh are the reasons he went there, then the man needs psychiatric counseling."

Is Baker an isolated, rogue element in the talk industry? Hardly. He remains on the air (toned down slightly)—and on the advisory board of the National Association of Radio Talk Show Hosts.

Reporting for *EXTRA!*, the magazine of the media watch group FAIR, Colorado journalist Leslie Jorgensen interviewed the executive director of the talk show host association. Jorgensen was told: "You're trying to put a muzzle on free speech.... Chuck Baker is a good host and knows how to talk to people and calm them down."

No one muzzles nationally syndicated talk host G. Gordon Liddy, who has also expressed sympathy for right-wing militias. Three days before Baker's show touted an armed march on Washington, Liddy told listeners how to kill federal Alcohol, Tobacco and Firearms agents: "They've got a big target on there, ATF. Don't shoot at that because they've got a vest on underneath that. Head shots, head shots." Later in the program, Liddy said: "Kill the sons of bitches."

Liddy's show is distributed by Westwood One, the country's biggest syndicator of radio programming.

In many cities, right-talk is not enough; the new marketing device in radio is "hot talk"—but it might be renamed "hate talk."

In Phoenix, KFYI "hot talk" host Bob Mohan declared that gun control advocate Sarah Brady "ought to be put down. A humane shot at a veterinarian's would be an easy way to do it."

In liberal San Francisco, KSFO—owned by the ABC/Capital Cities media giant—recently abandoned its diverse lineup of talk hosts, and switched to "hot talk": *all right, all the time*. Now San Franciscans can hear hosts who speak of "lynching a few liberals" and encourage listeners to "shoot illegal immigrants who come across the border" for reward money.

Let's face it: There's something wrong with the talk radio spectrum when Rush Limbaugh is starting to sound tolerant.

[This column appeared two months before the Oklahoma City bombing.]

February 15, 1995

NEXT TO THESE GUYS, RUSH SOUNDS LIKE-- WELL-- A TREE-HUGGING LIBERAL...
HEY, IF THE SPOTTED OWL CAN'T, LIKE, GROOVE WITH THE TIMBER INDUSTRY, MAN--
--THEN IT SHOULD, LIKE, MELLOW OUT!
YOU DIG?
TOM TOMORROW©5-10-95

Don't Need a Weatherman to Know Which Way Rush Blows

If you doubt that some media outlets put popularity and profits ahead of truth, just ask radio weatherman Sean Boyd.

Boyd was fired last month [April 1995] from his job at a Fresno, California, talk station. The firing came after he refused to distort his forecast for the day of KMJ Radio's annual Dittohead Picnic honoring Rush Limbaugh fans.

Boyd predicted a likelihood of rain, but his boss wanted him to say there was "an even greater chance of no showers." Thousands of Limbaugh devotees attended the picnic, and just as the Miss Dittohead swimsuit pageant began, they got drenched.

No one soaks the dittoheads with more misinformation than Rush Limbaugh himself. Yet, to hear the mighty talk-show host tell it, he offers his listeners the unvarnished facts not available from anyone but him—certainly not from the "liberal press."

Limbaugh's "don't trust the media" pose is a bit ironic given that it's the mass media that helped make him the country's most powerful political commentator. Besides his own shows on 900 radio and TV stations, he appears as a guest "expert" on leading TV news programs.

In mid-April [1995], Limbaugh was invited into the elite pundit club on *This Week With David Brinkley*—appearing alongside Cokie Roberts and George Will. Does ABC News think that Will needs help articulating a right-wing perspective?

Limbaugh's exalted media status stands as quite an indictment of today's national media.

Ted Koppel, for example, had Limbaugh on ABC's *Nightline* to offer his expertise about the environment.

Limbaugh's knowledge of the subject? He asserts that "styrofoam and plastic milk jugs are biodegradable!" He pooh-poohs the very real dangers of asbestos and dioxin. He proclaims that "there are more acres of forest land in America today" than in 1492—an error of a few hundred million acres.

On global warming, he blusters: "Even if polar ice caps melted, there would be no rise in ocean levels." Scientists say the rise in sea levels would be catastrophic.

Koppel also featured Limbaugh in May 1994 as part of a 90-minute ABC special on news coverage of the Whitewater scandal.

Limbaugh's expertise? Two months before the invite from Koppel, Limbaugh had told his TV audience of a media cover-up—that Whitewater "would be one of the biggest and most well-kept secrets" if not for Limbaugh and right-wing publications. Said Limbaugh: "I don't think the *New York Times* has run a story on [Whitewater] yet."

Here's an "expert" who couldn't recall that the *Times* BROKE the Whitewater story in March 1992. Nor that the *Times* had run six front-page articles on Whitewater in the two months prior to his cover-up charge.

In early 1994, Limbaugh's broadcasts repeatedly implied that the suicide of White House aide Vince Foster was really a murder. On March 10, for example, he urgently—and inaccurately—told his radio audience of a newsletter reporting that "Vince Foster was murdered in an apartment owned by Hillary Clinton."

Asked about the Foster suicide on the Koppel special, Limbaugh dissembled: "Never have I suggested that this was murder."

Weeks ago, he told his TV viewers that the press had ignored the Contract With America "all during the campaign." Declared Limbaugh: "The *New York Times* never ran anything on the Contract till after the election. The rest of the news media hardly talked about it at all."

Limbaugh depicted a big plot—except the facts were, as usual, wrong. A Nexis database search of newspapers shows over 1,300 articles mentioning the Contract before election day; 45 such articles appeared in the *Times*.

Rush Limbaugh has amassed political power and a following of millions through the daily deployment of conspiracy theories and distortions. He richly deserves the title "The Lyin' King." Yet he largely evades serious media scrutiny.

In 1954, Edward R. Murrow of CBS News confronted (and deflated) another demagogue allergic to facts and documentation: Sen. Joe McCarthy. How has CBS responded to the rise of Limbaugh? By trying to hire him as a commentator.

And what about the *New York Times*, so often the target of Limbaugh's phony charges? The *Times* chose Limbaugh to appear in TV ads for the newspaper.

Do facts matter to these media outlets, or is Limbaugh's huge following the only thing that counts?

May 24, 1995

Part IV
Conservatives Spin "Liberal" Media

If the media are so "liberal," why is it that so many conservative—even reactionary—viewpoints and movements have gained mass media acceptance in recent years?

The Power and Glory
of the Heritage Foundation

WASHINGTON—Based in a spacious brick building a few blocks from the Capitol, the Heritage Foundation is running the most effective media operation in American politics.

Heritage has succeeded with a savvy strategy: Raise a lot of money from rich people with a right-wing agenda. Hire writers, commentators and out-of-office politicians who share that agenda, and call them "fellows," "policy analysts" and "distinguished scholars." And, always, back them up with a public-relations juggernaut that's second to none.

The big money came easy. Back in 1973, beer baron Joseph Coors contributed a quarter-million dollars to get the project rolling. Since then, the megabucks have flowed in: from Amway Corp. and other firms, a slew of very conservative foundations, and wealthy families with names like Scaife, Mellon and Coors.

Though it boasts of enormous clout on Capitol Hill, the Heritage Foundation insists that it doesn't "lobby"—a necessary denial to retain tax-exempt standing with the IRS. But consider these comments from Heritage vice presidents published in its 1995 Annual Report: "Heritage has been involved in crafting almost every piece of major legislation to move through Congress... Without exaggeration, I think we've in effect become Congress's unofficial research arm."

With the help of its tax-exempt status, Heritage raised $29.7 million in 1995. Core funding came from just a few places; 31 checks from donors like the Olin Foundation and the Bradley Foundation accounted for $8.5 million.

Heritage has a long history of receiving large donations from overseas. It continues to rake in at least several hundred thousand dollars from Taiwan and South Korea each year.

According to a document uncovered by members of South Korea's National Assembly in autumn 1988, Korean intelligence gave $2.2 million to the Heritage Foundation on the sly during the early 1980s. Heritage officials "categorically deny" the accusation.

Heritage's latest annual report does acknowledge a $400,000 grant from the Korean conglomerate Samsung. Another donor, the Korea Foundation—which conduits money from the South Korean government—has given Heritage almost $1 million in the past three years. However, U.S. media outlets rarely allude to Heritage's financial links with Korea, even when such ties are directly relevant to the story.

The *New York Times* avoided the subject in a March 12 [1996] news article about two former South Korean presidents on trial for the massacre of hundreds of pro-democracy demonstrators at Kwangju in 1980. The article merely said that the pair's attorney "quoted from a report by the Heritage Foundation, the conservative American research institute, referring to the protesters in Kwangju not as democracy campaigners but as 'rioters.'"

Likewise, on April 9, a *Washington Post* dispatch cited the views of Daryl Plunk, "a Korea specialist at the conservative Heritage Foundation"—but made no mention of monetary ties between South Korea and Heritage.

By now, the Heritage Foundation is the most widely quoted and sound-bitten think tank in the U.S. media (as documented in a new FAIR survey). Appearing frequently on television and radio, Heritage personnel also write many commentaries for newspapers and magazines. Meanwhile, Heritage produces a blizzard of press releases, position papers, news conferences and seminars aired on C-SPAN.

Since 1977, Vice President Herb Berkowitz and Public Relations Counsel Hugh Newton have coordinated Heritage's nonstop media barrage. Like gunslingers blowing smoke from the barrels of their six-shooters, they're glad to recount how so many notches got in their media belts.

Until 1980, Heritage Foundation was just another Washington group funded with piles of money from wealthy interests. "Ronald Reagan's election changed a lot—made us

much more important," Newton told us. Berkowitz added: "They rode in, we had the bible ready."

The "bible" was a Heritage report—"Mandate for Leadership"—calling for deregulation of business, deep cuts in social programs and huge spending hikes for the Pentagon. President Reagan adopted it as the blueprint for his administration.

Today, Heritage works closely with the Republican congressional majority. "Heritage is without question the most far-reaching conservative organization in the country in the war of ideas," Newt Gingrich declared in a November 1994 speech.

But, in his book *The News Shapers*, professor Lawrence Soley of Marquette University notes that "among beltway think tanks, Heritage associates have the weakest scholarly credentials." Instead of seeking quality, "the Heritage Foundation appears to strive for quantity"—feeding a glut of material to Congress and the news media. "The biggest names at this think tank," Soley adds, "are not thinkers, but former Republican officials." (Highly paid "fellows" have included Jack Kemp, Edwin Meese and William Bennett.)

One author who researches the far right, Russ Bellant, describes the Heritage Foundation as "less a traditional think tank...than a propaganda center that creates justifications for pre-conceived positions and then professionally packages the results in a format palatable to politicians and the press."

Such criticisms don't seem to bother the men in charge of public relations for the Heritage Foundation. They look quite satisfied.

April 24, 1996

Mass Media
Help Boost Promise Keepers

So far, news coverage of Promise Keepers has been more like advertising than journalism.

Big media outlets jumped on the Promise Keepers bandwagon last year [1995]. ABC News lauded "a Christian men's movement devoted to reviving faith and family." An upbeat *New York Times* story appeared under the front-page headline "Men Crowd Stadiums to Fulfill Their Souls." *Time* magazine chimed in with an equally gushy article titled "Full of Promise."

The current [July/August 1996] *Saturday Evening Post* provides the typical spin: "Promise Keepers is striking a chord with today's men, who are seeking to reclaim and strengthen their roles as husbands, fathers and community leaders."

Promise Keepers drew a total of 727,000 men to its huge gatherings in 1995 and expects to attract more than 1 million this year. The sincerity of most participants is unmistakable.

However, so is the rigid power of the organization's hierarchy.

The Promise Keeper dogma insists that husbands should lead and wives should follow—a message proclaimed at one stadium-filling event after another. Less obvious is the leadership's hostility to gay people.

The group's founder and most revered leader, former University of Colorado football coach Bill McCartney, campaigned for a statewide anti-gay ballot measure in 1992. He told a Colorado press conference that homosexuality is "an abomination of almighty God."

When they claim to be nonpolitical, Promise Keeper chieftains are obscuring reality. The far-right powerhouse Focus on the Family helped to bankroll the organization and continues to publish its main text, *Seven Promises of a Promise Keeper*.

James Dobson, head of Focus on the Family, has been a Promise Keepers speaker. Another big supporter, Christian

Coalition eminence Pat Robertson, has featured McCartney on his *700 Club* TV program.

Although mass media tell us little about the nitty-gritty of Promise Keepers, we can now get a much clearer picture—thanks to researchers and independent journalists who have rushed in where mainstream reporters fear to tread:

- The August [1996] issue of *The Progressive* magazine scrutinizes the Promise Keepers. "Their first step is to reassert male dominance in the family," writes Nancy Novosad. A companion article by Suzanne Pharr describes Promise Keepers as "ground troops in an authoritarian movement that seeks to merge church and state."

- The Aug. 5 edition of *In These Times* calls Promise Keeper events "the slickest religious consumer product since televangelism." Frederick Clarkson observes that "an ambitious political and religious agenda...lurks behind the pep-rally atmosphere."

- Ending racial division is a strong Promise Keepers theme. But, in her new book *Facing the Wrath*, scholar Sara Diamond notes what's missing: "Rhetoric around 'racial reconciliation' typically does not mention the political-economic roots of racial injustice." That brand of anti-racism serves the strategy of the Christian right—"which wants to absolve itself of the racist stereotype and enlist black and Latino conservatives who oppose abortion, gay rights and affirmative action."

- In another recent book (*Eyes Right!*), researcher Russ Bellant says that Promise Keepers "may be the strongest, most organized effort to capitalize on male backlash in the country during the 1990s."

- A video documentary and a printed report, produced by the Manhattan-based Sterling Research Associates, go beyond the standard media accounts. They place Promise Keepers in context as "a major effort by the leadership of well-financed religious conservative organizations to create a new men-only movement to promote their social and political agenda."

As more information surfaces about Promise Keepers, some activists are trying to raise key issues. A few weeks ago—when nearly 50,000 men converged on a Charlotte, N.C., speedway for a Promise Keepers extravaganza—the president of Liberals United held a news conference outside the gates to confront the group's ideology. Charlotte native T. J. Walker, who now lives in New York City, returned to his hometown to speak out against male supremacy and anti-gay bigotry.

Such responses seem likely to grow. As Promise Keepers readied another mega-event, this time at a university stadium in Eugene, Oregon, a local coalition announced plans for a candlelight vigil outside the stadium to take a stand for equal rights.

For years, the leaders of Promise Keepers have enjoyed plenty of favorable media coverage. Now, their critics are clamoring to be heard.

July 31, 1996

Promise Keepers rally on Fort Bragg army base

Bill Bennett's Hypocrisy
Is No Virtue

Just when you thought gangsta rap music, Geraldo and Jenny Jones were devouring the soul of American civilization, here comes a savior—the ever-virtuous William Bennett.

Sometimes the cure is worse than the disease.

Bennett, a former secretary of education and drug czar, once aspired to be president. That requires getting elected. Guardians of national virtue are self-appointed.

When you see Bennett in the media—he's hard to miss these days—promoting the Republican agenda or his book on morality, or leading his new campaign against trashy daytime TV talk shows, you'd be well-advised to remember his occupation: politician.

Like other skilled politicians today, Bennett has a finely honed ability to seize upon issues and garner big media attention—all the while masking his essential contradictions and failure to generate solutions.

Take the issue of TV's sleazy, sex-saturated talk shows—profit-mad programs that are going deeper into the gutter at the same time that a half-dozen giant corporations gain increasing dominion over the TV industry.

If you don't believe there's a connection between these two trends, ask Phil Donahue. He's the pioneer in daytime talk TV, who now finds himself off the air in New York City and elsewhere—replaced by shows that aspire to an all-smut-all-the-time format.

Donahue sees media monopolization as a key factor in the dominance of sleaze—and the shrinking of diverse voices and issues on television.

Behind each oily talk-show host is a media conglomerate—Jenny Jones (Time Warner), Gordon Elliott (Rupert Murdoch/Fox), Geraldo Rivera (Tribune Co.), Montel Williams and Maury Povich

(Paramount/Viacom), Ricki Lake (Sony), Jerry Springer and Sally Jessy Raphael (Multimedia/Gannett).

It's quite a feat of hypocrisy for a politician like Bennett to target TV talk hosts, after his Republican allies in Congress just passed a telecommunications "reform" bill giving unprecedented monopoly powers to the same corporations polluting the airwaves.

Public attacks on Ricki Lake and Montel Williams may play well with conservative activists. But Bennett might accomplish more through private talks with Senator Bob Dole and House Speaker Newt Gingrich—rebuking their efforts to bestow still more power on media cartels that put ratings above all else. (He could also ask his political allies to return the campaign donations they receive from the corporations behind TV filth.)

If the "free market" points the way to our mass-media future, then trash TV has only just begun.

Meanwhile, there's more than a little hypocrisy in Bennett denouncing violence in rap and prurience on television, when his party has led the charge for years to de-fund and destroy public TV—the one broadcast television network that's almost free of violence and prurient sex.

There's also duplicity in Bennett's adroit selection of media targets. While raging against daytime talk television, he avoids criticism of another talk medium—also rife with vulgarity—which has played a big role in building the clout of Bennett and other conservatives. That medium is talk radio.

One of the strongest voices in all of talk radio is New York's Bob Grant, who abuses callers and uses racist, often violent rhetoric.

Bennett waxes eloquent when he criticizes rap songs in which fictional characters seem to revel in gang violence and killings. But he goes silent on Grant, who is distinctly *non-fiction* when he expresses his wish that New York police machine gun gay-pride marchers. Or when Grant says: "I'd like to get every environmentalist, put 'em up against a wall, and shoot 'em."

Bennett has paid for political ads on Grant's program—and Grant boasts that Bennett has appeared several times on his show.

At Bennett's Oct. 26 [1995] news conference on trash TV, criticism was leveled at an episode titled "Get Bigger Breasts or Else." Last year, Rush Limbaugh used more than one broadcast to wail: "We're in bad shape in this country when you can't look at a couple of huge knockers and notice it."

Is Bennett rankled by Rush Limbaugh's lewd comments about women? Does he find it less than virtuous that Limbaugh mocked a 13-year-old Chelsea Clinton as "the White House dog"? Apparently not—since Bennett has praised Limbaugh as "possibly our greatest living American."

Don't expect consistency from a man who is more politician than media critic.

During a recent TV show, we pressed a spokesperson from Bennett's "Empower America" organization as to why he was ignoring talk radio filth. The response was that Bennett needed to focus on one issue at a time.

The day Bennett takes on Rush Limbaugh is the day we risk heart attacks. Luckily for our health, that day is a long way off. Indeed, the evidence suggests that Bennett would not be targeting Ricki, Jenny and Montel if they were as helpful to Republican power as radio talkmeisters Rush, G. Gordon and Bob Grant.

William Bennett says he's trying to organize resistance to "the giant popular culture sleaze machine." But it's hard to oppose a machine that helps fund your political allies. Especially when you subscribe to a "free enterprise" ideology that equates the public good with the unrestrained pursuit of profit.

November 1, 1995

Part V
"Public Broadcasting" Tunes Out the Public

Disgusted with commercial media outlets, many people have turned to public stations for news and public-affairs coverage. But external and internal pressures have taken their toll—and, by now, there's not much of the public left in "public broadcasting."

Save Public Television:
Pull the Plug on PBS Bureaucrats

It's the bombast season again in Washington as another debate over public broadcasting blows hot and blustery—with both sides promoting bogus claims.

While Republicans move to cut federal funds for public TV and radio, public broadcasting executives declare their dedication to balanced, noncommercial programming.

First, let's review the nonsense coming from right-wing critics.

"One of the things we're going to do this year, I hope," says Newt Gingrich, "is to zero out the Corporation for Public Broadcasting, which has been eating taxpayers' money."

"Eating taxpayers' money" to the feeble tune of about $1 per American each year, CPB disburses $286 million of federal money to public broadcasting, for program production and local stations. The federal government, which devotes almost $200 million yearly to military bands, spends far less on public broadcasting than most Western European countries.

Let's privatize public TV and sell off CPB to private business, say Gingrich and his allies.

In fact, public television is virtually privatized *already*. Take PBS's *MacNeil/Lehrer NewsHour*, long underwritten by such companies as Pepsico and Archer Daniels Midland. Last month [December 1994], two-thirds of MacNeil/Lehrer Productions was purchased by a subsidiary of TCI, the cable TV giant.

Today, corporations contribute more to public television than the federal government does. With grants earmarked for specific programs, large businesses and foundations increasingly determine which "public TV" programs are produced—and which aren't. Thanks to big money backers, William F. Buckley's *Firing Line* is a PBS institution, though it has few viewers. But controversial or anti-establishment programs with sizable audiences have been dropped—for lack of a corporate sponsor ("underwriter" in PBS jargon).

Public TV is biased toward the left, Republicans claim.

A 1993 MacArthur Foundation study of public affairs programming on PBS proved just the opposite. Counting the occasional Bill Moyers special or leftish documentary, PBS stations on a weekly basis tilt heavily toward conservative and corporate views. Three regular programs cover the business agenda—*Nightly Business Report*, *Adam Smith's Money World* and Louis Rukeyser's *Wall $treet Week*; none cover the agendas of groups that often conflict with big business, whether labor, consumer or environmental.

Bill Buckley's is one of three weekly politics shows hosted by rightists; none are hosted by leftists. The one weekly PBS program aimed at African-Americans—*Tony Brown's Journal* —is hosted by a Republican. And, studies document, middle-of-the-road shows like *MacNeil/Lehrer* are also biased toward elite opinion.

Republicans on Capitol Hill are savvy enough to have learned that the more they pressure PBS every year or two (threatening to cut funds), the more conservative the programming gets. Former Reagan speechwriter Peggy Noonan, for example, will soon be hosting her own PBS miniseries; last year, neo-conservative Ben Wattenberg launched his weekly show, *Think Tank*, funded by right-wing foundations.

Which brings us to the hypocritical rhetoric emanating from Washington's PBS bureaucrats. Now fighting for their jobs, Ervin Duggan and Richard Carlson, the presidents of PBS and CPB, have voiced unswerving support for noncommercialism and for TV accessible to working people and the poor. Duggan recently blasted a "tawdry popular culture, driven by market place values."

But in the last year, national PBS executives have lavishly funded a weekly game show while shunning weekly programs like *Rights & Wrongs* (about global human rights) and *We Do The Work* (about workers and unions). They've repeatedly rejected Oscar-winning documentaries—most recently *Defending Our Lives*, about battered women. Meanwhile, corporate ads on PBS keep growing longer—now nearly indistinguishable from those on the "tawdry" commercial networks.

Because they've made decision after decision putting the needs of corporate donors ahead of viewers ill-served by commercial TV, the PBS bureaucrats now lack vital constituencies that could be fighting in their behalf.

Beyond the shallow debate in Washington, possible solutions exist—if we can build a new *locally controlled, financially independent* structure for public broadcasting. What's needed is more public, and less private, money.

Here's how: Although Newt Gingrich never challenges the huge subsidy that taxpayers provide to *private* TV and radio stations, the federal license to broadcast is like a license to print money. If these stations paid a commensurate license fee, big funds could be collected for noncommercial broadcasting. A tax on commercials could also reap millions. Such measures would ensure steady funding that politicians couldn't obstruct.

Who should get the money? Local public stations—with democratically elected boards. Adequately funded stations would find or produce the programming that suits the diverse needs of their local communities—needs unmet by commercial stations.

For those of us who believe in the promise of public television, maybe it's time to pull the plug on the national PBS bureaucracy.

January 18, 1995

MacNeil/Lehrer NewsHour at 20:
Hold the Cheers

As the *MacNeil/Lehrer NewsHour* prepares to mark its 20th anniversary, press releases are hailing the PBS program as "one of the most influential news sources in the world." But from where we sit—in front of the TV screen—that's no cause for celebration.

Aired on more than 300 TV stations in the United States, *MacNeil/Lehrer* has a nightly audience of 5 million people. Meanwhile, the program reaches viewers around the globe via satellite networks—including the official U.S. Information Agency's "WorldNet" system.

With the *NewsHour* poised to enter a third decade, some changes are underway. In late October [1995], longtime co-anchor Robert MacNeil will leave the program, which is being renamed the *NewsHour With Jim Lehrer*. And MacNeil/Lehrer Productions is hoping to start a second nightly news broadcast, for an 11 p.m. slot, on the nation's public TV stations.

"We will bring the very same standards to the new program that we've been using on the *MacNeil/Lehrer NewsHour*," the president of MacNeil/Lehrer Productions, Al Vecchione, told us in a recent interview.

His words were meant to be reassuring. But they sounded ominous to us.

PBS viewers hardly need another national news program with "the very same standards."

The media watch group we're associated with, FAIR, conducted a detailed study of every *MacNeil/Lehrer NewsHour* program during a six-month period in 1989. Among the findings:

- The program's guest list was chock full of think-tank "experts" from conservative, corporate-funded outfits— in particular, the Center for Strategic and International Studies and the American Enterprise Institute, which had

14 appearances between them. In contrast, analysts from various progressive think tanks never appeared.

- Nine-tenths of the U.S. guests on *MacNeil/Lehrer* were white, and 87 percent were male.

- Almost half—46 percent—of the U.S. guests were current or former government officials. However, only 6 percent of the guests were from public-interest groups (such as consumer-rights, civil-rights and labor organizations) critical of government policies.

- The program exhibited a knack for having discussions about the environment while excluding environmentalists. Only one of 17 guests on environment-related segments was a representative of an environmental group.

- In seven *MacNeil/Lehrer* discussion segments on Central America, all 22 guests were either U.S. officials or representatives of U.S.-allied governments in the region. No one was invited from the U.S. mass movement against military intervention.

Overall, the *MacNeil/Lehrer NewsHour* has excelled at serving as a nightly transmission belt for official opinion. Most of the time, disagreements are well within the range to be found among powerful politicians and lobbyists in Washington.

No wonder the show has been repeatedly praised as "balanced" by rightist groups—like Accuracy in Media and the National Conservative Political Action Conference—which normally bash network TV news for being too "liberal."

The man soon to become chief anchor of the *NewsHour*, Jim Lehrer, has little patience with calls for genuine diversity. Former *NewsHour* staffers have told us that Lehrer dismisses progressive policy critics as "moaners" and "whiners" unfit to appear on the show.

The response was similar when we asked the president of MacNeil/Lehrer Productions to comment on charges that the *NewsHour* lacks diversity. "I think that's an outrageous criticism of our program," Al Vecchione replied. "It's in a class by itself in terms of being fair and even-handed."

Introspection is not a strong suit at the *NewsHour*.

But then again, those who pay the media piper tend to call the tune—not every note, but the prevailing melody.

From the outset, the program has depended on corporate "underwriters" for major chunks of its financing. In the past, these underwriters have included AT&T and Pepsico. This year, two politically active firms—the agribusiness giant Archer Daniels Midland and the New York Life Insurance Co.—account for about $11 million, nearly half of the program's budget.

The show's producers, of course, are quick to proclaim total independence from funders. But the companies funneling money to the most important show on PBS have reason to be pleased with their investments. Few of the program's 15,000 minutes of news coverage each year are likely to cause anything approaching distress in corporate suites.

When a subsidiary of the private media-conglomerate TCI purchased two-thirds of MacNeil/Lehrer Productions last year, PBS network president Ervin Duggan promptly called it "a welcome infusion of capital into the *NewsHour*."

These days, it seems odd to hear PBS referred to as "public television" when the funding—and content—of its public affairs programming are so dominated by private, for-profit, big-money institutions.

So we won't be cheering as the *NewsHour* begins its 21st year. And we won't be hoping that MacNeil/Lehrer Productions is successful in its plans to team up with the *Wall Street Journal* to create another national news show.

The new program would draw 90 percent of its funding from outside corporate underwriters. And the show would be owned by a pair of private media powers—Dow Jones & Co. and TCI. All in all, it's a remarkable concept for "public" television.

September 27, 1995

Bob Dole and Public Television:
Killing It Softly

Four years ago, Bob Dole was a roaring tiger on the subject of public television. As the Senate's most powerful critic of PBS, he accused the network of "unrelenting liberal cheerleading" and charged that "apologists are hiding behind Big Bird, Mr. Rogers and *Masterpiece Theatre*."

In 1996, however, Dole's fierce rhetoric against PBS is gone. He's even purring a bit. A few weeks ago, at a Capitol Hill meeting with lobbyists for public television and radio, Dole staffers offered his support for setting up a federal trust fund to provide stable subsidies.

Dole's current stance is prudent for his presidential campaign. After all, defenders of public broadcasting have proven their strength. Last year—when some congressional Republicans vowed to "zero out" federal funds for public broadcasters—a nationwide uprising from viewers and listeners forced GOP leaders to backtrack in a hurry.

But retreat should not be confused with surrender. There's more than one way to kill public broadcasting. It can be murdered outright—or gradually strangled by corporate embraces with the aid of government. The latter process is well underway.

"Over a period of many years, the external pressure from Congress has induced a sort of self-censorship on the part of PBS," says Ruby Lerner, executive director of the 5,000-member Association of Independent Video and Filmmakers. "The network has gotten very cautious about what they're going to air. They don't want to be harassed by politicians who are, in turn, harassed by a lot of the organizations on the right."

Federal funds, channeled through the Corporation for Public Broadcasting, have always been sparse. CPB outlays now amount to about $1 a year for every U.S. citizen, with a projected annual drop of a few cents until 1999. Tight budgets have bolstered arguments that more corporate money is needed to sustain public broadcasting.

Today, you won't see much of the public on "public television." None of the regular PBS programs, for instance, is devoted to exploring the lives of working people; not one is devoted to civil-rights or environmental or consumer activism.

Meanwhile, huge companies keep pouring serious money into public TV programs they appreciate, such as the *McLaughlin Group* shoutfest, *Wall $treet Week*, *Washington Week in Review* and the *Nightly Business Report*—literally made possible by corporate backing.

Each edition of the *NewsHour With Jim Lehrer* includes a pair of colorful pitches for agribusiness giant Archer Daniels Midland, "supermarket to the world." Likewise, on a daily basis, National Public Radio airs flattering descriptions of ADM. Those "enhanced underwriter credits" symbolize the steady privatization of public broadcasting.

ADM pays $5.8 million a year to the *NewsHour*. It also gives plenty of money to NPR for *All Things Considered*—but the radio network won't say how much. A secretive policy exists "as a courtesy to our underwriter," NPR spokesperson Pat Lute told us in a May 22 [1996] interview. Notice: NPR's courtesy to ADM outweighs informing the public about "public radio."

A highly political firm with billions of dollars riding on public perceptions and legislation, ADM has gained enormously from a federal ethanol subsidy averaging $500 million per year during the past decade. But don't hold your breath for the *NewsHour* or *All Things Considered* to broadcast a series of investigative reports about ADM—the world's biggest producer of ethanol.

Bob Dole is hardly inclined to complain that public broadcasting is on the take from Archer Daniels Midland and other business titans. As it happens, Dole's campaign committees have received $227,800 from ADM, which was also kind enough to give him a lift on its corporate jets at least 35 times.

For many programming executives, deference to the private sector has become so routine that it seems normal, even wise. In the process, big checks determine more and more of what's on the air.

These days, the public-broadcasting elites and Bob Dole share a roughly similar vision for the future: Federal appropriations will slowly dwindle. Stepping into the breach more than ever will be corporate America. It's a perfect scenario for winning bipartisan applause in Washington. The only losers will be Americans who want public broadcasting in fact as well as in name.

May 22, 1996

Part VI
Health in the Marketplace

From the production of cigarettes to the spread of pollution to the cutthroat stratagems of medical conglomerates, much of the routine media coverage we get is hazardous to public health.

In Disneyland, Journalism
Means Saying You're Sorry

Only a few weeks have passed since the Walt Disney Co. announced its takeover of ABC—but already the TV network is living up to the Mickey Mouse image.

In a cowardly capitulation, ABC has settled a defamation suit brought by cigarette giants Philip Morris and R.J. Reynolds.

ABC used its national airwaves to apologize to the tobacco companies not once, not twice, but three times—including on *Monday Night Football*.

The network also agreed to pay millions of dollars to cover the legal bills of the tobacco lawyers. (The settlement apparently didn't include a pledge to dangle cigarettes from the mouths of Disney's cartoon characters.)

For journalists, ABC's surrender was a white flag seen 'round the world—dramatizing the awesome power that big-money firms can wield with lawsuits and other threats against investigative reporting. It also dramatized the weakened position of working journalists at today's huge media/entertainment companies, which are expanding through merger and acquisition.

Let's face it: To most owners of national media, serious journalism is a nuisance. It costs money, takes time and doesn't always deliver top ratings. And when your staff engages in tough reporting about corporate interests, they can retaliate.

Sometimes those interests are major sponsors. Philip Morris can't advertise cigarettes on the air, but it does hawk dozens of products from its Kraft General Foods and Miller Brewing subsidiaries. Along with filing suit against ABC, Philip Morris also threatened to withdraw advertising on that network—an annual tab of $100 million.

(R.J. Reynolds Tobacco is a subsidiary of RJR Nabisco, which sells food products and is a leading TV advertiser. In this media environment, it's not easy for the activist group

INFACT to publicize its consumer boycott of RJR Nabisco and Philip Morris products.)

The $10 billion defamation suit stemmed from an in-depth and overwhelmingly accurate Feb. 28, 1994, report on ABC's *Day One* program, documenting how cigarette companies "control levels of nicotine"—the ingredient that keeps smokers addicted.

Documentation in the 13-minute segment came from internal tobacco-industry memos, a former R.J. Reynolds manager (interviewed in silhouette), current Reynolds scientists, tobacco processors and an independent research lab hired by ABC.

Reporter John Martin began by pointing out that cigarettes are not simply "leaves rolled in white paper"—but "a scientifically engineered product."

Martin proceeded to detail how cigarettes are made from tobacco leaves and a filler known as "reconstituted tobacco," produced by grinding tobacco stalks and stems. In the process, nicotine is removed—which would be good news for smokers trying to kick their addiction.

The bad news, as ABC showed, is that nicotine from tobacco extract is then added back into the cigarette. According to the former R. J. Reynolds manager, it can be added in virtually any strength.

Martin got a Reynolds scientist to admit that the company could produce cigarettes with all the nicotine removed. "How tobacco companies manipulate nicotine and their reluctance to take it out," concluded Martin, "strongly suggests that they want smokers to get nicotine."

The ABC segment quoted from a once-secret 1972 memo in which a Philip Morris official wrote: "Think of the cigarette pack as a storage container for a day's supply of nicotine. Think of the cigarette as a dispenser for a dose unit of nicotine."

The segment, which included tobacco industry responses, also assessed the politics of tobacco on Capitol Hill—quoting a health official who described Congress's role in specially exempting cigarettes from "every major health legislation since 1964": the Hazardous Substances Act, Controlled Substances Act, Consumer Products Safety Act, etc.

To win this defamation case at trial, the tobacco firms would have had the difficult task of proving recklessness or dishonesty by ABC journalists. On the subject of honesty, remember that the chief executives of seven cigarette companies testified before Congress last year that nicotine is *not* addictive.

The trial, which might have shed needed light on the secretive cigarette-manufacturing process, was likely to focus on one disputed word: reporter Martin's statement that cigarettes are "spiked" with nicotine. But that word was factually explained in full context by ABC's report.

We haven't found a single ABC journalist who supports the network's apologetic settlement of the suit. Why settle, even in a tobacco-friendly court in Richmond, when the broadcast was fair and accurate?

Journalists had reason to see a sell-out in a management apology—"we should not have reported that Philip Morris and Reynolds add significant amounts of nicotine from outside sources"—repenting for claims ABC's news story never made. Martin and producer Walt Bogdanich refused to sign the settlement.

Given that the well-documented *Day One* report helped prod the Food and Drug Administration to consider action against the tobacco industry for dispensing a drug, it made some sense for cigarette makers to file suit as a PR counter attack. The ABC apology now gives them a huge propaganda victory.

But why did ABC settle? One goal was to smooth the way for the Disney merger. As the *Wall Street Journal* reported, ABC general counsel and vice president Alan Braverman (the driving force behind the network's cave-in) had told Disney's lawyers during merger negotiations that he believed ABC and Philip Morris "could work out a settlement."

ABC's capitulation will probably invite more lawsuits by powerful interests with the money to intimidate. It could also make mainstream journalists a bit more shy about investigating deadly enterprises like the tobacco industry.

And that's not Mickey Mouse.

August 23, 1995

Shrugging Off an Attack
on the Clean Air Act

The news should have caused a national uproar: A global trade authority ordered the United States to allow higher levels of air pollution or pay huge fines. But, if you blinked, you may have missed the story entirely.

In a decision with momentous implications, the new World Trade Organization ruled that the U.S. law known as the Clean Air Act is unacceptable because of restrictions it places on pollutants in imported gasoline. The decree could result in higher levels of toxic auto emissions.

"This is a major blow to the ability of the United States to protect public health," said a senior attorney for the Natural Resources Defense Council.

But, when the news broke in mid-January [1996], it was a fleeting blip on the media screen. Since then, follow-up coverage has been almost impossible to find.

Why did such a dramatic—and important—story drop from sight so quickly? Because none of this nation's top movers and shakers wanted to make a big deal out of it.

The White House preferred that the story disappear, pronto. After all, the World Trade Organization owes its existence to the GATT trade pact that President Clinton pushed through Congress in late 1994.

Back then, Clinton vowed that the accord would not interfere with U.S. anti-pollution laws. His trade representative, Mickey Kantor, even claimed that the GATT agreement "will help improve environmental protection."

Yet, in the wake of the WTO's outrageous ruling Jan. 17, leading Republicans were not well-positioned to turn it into a campaign issue.

Sen. Bob Dole has lamented the enormous power of the WTO, but there's no escaping the reality that he voted to create it in the first place. So did Phil Gramm and Richard Lugar, the other senators seeking the GOP presidential nomination. And publishing magnate Steve Forbes has always been enthusiastic.

In fact, among this year's major party candidates for president, only Patrick Buchanan opposed the GATT treaty. And he has a tough time sounding righteous about the WTO's assault on the Clean Air Act.

Buchanan loves to make passionate speeches about American sovereignty, but he happens to despise federal regulations that protect the environment. In keeping with his brand of political theology, Buchanan defines environmentalism as the antithesis of all that's holy. "Easter's gone," he declares angrily. "Now it's Earth Day. We can all go out and worship dirt."

On Capitol Hill, most Democrats—eager to cover for Clinton—are remaining silent about the WTO's action. This makes for notable hypocrisy. For instance, the newest member of the Senate, Oregon's Ron Wyden, has presented himself as a Democratic defender of ecology since his recent election to fill the unexpired term of Sen. Bob Packwood.

Republicans in Congress are "just going on a bender with respect to clean air, clean water and environmental laws," Wyden charged. Unfortunately, Wyden—who helped to establish the WTO by voting for the GATT agreement in the House—failed to denounce the WTO for going on a bender with respect to the Clean Air Act.

Stymied by public opinion that has forced congressional Republicans to back off from efforts to gut laws like the Clean Air Act, many corporate polluters now view the World Trade Organization as a godsend.

Multinational oil companies are quietly savoring the WTO's decision. They see big dollar signs ahead, with surging U.S. imports of dirty gasoline from outmoded foreign refineries.

What about environmental organizations? The sad truth is that the largest ones have gotten into the habit of muting their voices in deference to the White House.

One of the most independent advocacy groups—Public Citizen, founded by Ralph Nader—has not minced words. "Under the WTO, countries and their democratically elected representatives are very limited in what they can do to implement and enforce environmental objectives," says Lori Wallach, director of the group's Global Trade Watch.

Because of the WTO ruling on gasoline, Wallach told us, the United States must make "an unacceptable choice between allowing more polluted air or facing enormous sanctions—$150 million a year."

Welcome to global "free trade," WTO style.

After extolling the creation of the World Trade Organization, big media outlets have a responsibility to examine the threat it now poses to environmental safeguards.

Too often, debates over trade policy seem ideological or theoretical. But there's nothing abstract about the air we breathe.

[In June 1996, the Clinton administration agreed to comply with the WTO decision, pledging to change how the U.S. government applies environmental regulations to imported gasoline.]

February 7, 1996

Health Coverage:
The Emerging Scandal

The future of American health care may depend on the news media in 1996.

A recent flare of brilliant journalism could turn out to be a flash in the pan—or a guiding light for reporters and editors across the country. What's badly needed is illumination of the huge medical institutions known as HMOs.

The number of Americans enrolled in "health maintenance organizations" has more than doubled since 1986. Upward of 50 million people now rely on HMOs; most are run for profit.

From here to the horizon, the trend is clear: More of us will be getting our medical care from HMOs as they continue to expand and merge. We'll be able to choose from just a few HMO giants.

The outlines of the HMO future are already visible in a "managed care" landscape where the bottom line is superceding the Hippocratic oath.

"In managed care, profit comes from enrolling patients, not from spending money on them," says Dr. Steffie Woolhandler of Harvard Medical School. She warns of "a deep ethical swamp."

Last fall, the tabloid *New York Post*—ordinarily a stranger to quality journalism—ran a well-documented series under top-of-the-eye-chart headlines like "Outrage At HMOs."

While HMOs have some advantages—such as relatively low premiums for individuals and employers—the downsides are apt to be steep. One result: a ground swell of anger among patients and health practitioners.

Now, *Time* magazine has produced a breakthrough with an eight-page investigative piece in its January 22 [1996] issue. Titled "The Soul of an HMO," the article shows in painful detail how cost-cutting edicts from HMO managements put doctors in a box—and, all too often, shove patients up against an unyielding bureaucratic wall.

According to *Time*, managed care is "raising the question of whether patients, especially those with severe illnesses, can still trust their doctors."

Faced with directives to help maximize profits, many physicians are under constant pressure to shift their allegiance from patients to company stockholders.

Patients seeking care are liable to encounter delays and obstructions. As *Time* reports, the HMO process requires that "considerations other than mere health are brought to bear by corporate managers who must approve even such minor procedures as blood tests and mammograms."

When we spoke with *Time* senior writer Erik Larson, who authored the article, he emphasized that the proliferation of for-profit HMOs is central to the worsening plights of health-care consumers. It is symbolic, he said, that HMO managements routinely refer to the cost of actually providing health care as the "medical loss ratio."

In the upper reaches of HMOs, the lingo certainly tilts toward the fiscal. When we contacted Health Net, a large managed-care firm skewered in the *Time* story, we were referred to spokesperson David Olson. His official title? "Vice president of investor relations."

Olson denounced the *Time* article as "agenda journalism" —and added that he was in touch with other managed-care executives to discuss how to counteract the bad press: "As an industry, we have to start fighting back."

But managed-care corporations have never been idle on the public-relations front. Eager to boost enrollments, HMOs have been blitzing many communities with warm and cuddly outreach, ranging from slick brochures to billboards and television commercials.

Naturally, the advertised HMOs sound great. Few of us have the patience to scrutinize—much less comprehend—their fine print.

What the billboards and TV ads don't divulge is that many doctors and other health-care providers are afraid to speak out publicly. Larson—a former *Wall Street Journal* reporter who has written one book about handguns and another about corporate surveillance of American consumers—told us that he had never encountered as much fear among sources as he did while interviewing doctors for his *Time* article about HMOs.

"Doctors are petrified of saying anything about HMOs," Larson said. Many have signed contracts requiring them not to disclose information that might shake public confidence.

But some physicians have spoken out. Appearing on *Donahue* several weeks ago, Dr. David Himmelstein explained that "one of the HMOs that I practice in tells me I can't tell my patients if there's something wrong [with what] the HMO insists I do." Three days after the TV show, the HMO—U.S. Healthcare— abruptly canceled its contract with him.

The retribution did not silence Himmelstein. He told one reporter that numerous HMOs "offer doctors steep financial incentives—what I consider bribes—to minimize care."

Himmelstein teamed up with Woolhandler to write a scathing editorial about HMOs in the December 21 [1995] edition of the *New England Journal of Medicine*. They noted that "many patients...object to the transparent incentives for providing too little care."

Indeed. Many patients are seething as they discover what managed care portends for themselves and their loved ones.

The HMO onslaught "kind of snuck up on everybody" during the last few years, Larson commented. "I don't think the press was aware of the turmoil that managed care was bringing."

Today—like health care providers, consumers and public officials—journalists face the imperative of playing catch-up as the HMO juggernaut rolls on.

January 24, 1996

Part VII
Affirmative Re-Action

For a long time now, many media voices have called for ending programs designed to counter the continuing effects of unequal opportunity in our society. The success of the backlash is evident.

The Backlash
Against Affirmative Action

With political winds howling against affirmative action, many supporters seem to be backpedaling and running for cover. Opponents, meanwhile, keep raging against "reverse discrimination."

In the midst of the gathering storm, American journalism is doing little to provide clarity. No wonder Republican strategists look forward to using affirmative action as a "wedge issue."

Often misreported as a "quota" system, affirmative action involves special efforts in hiring and college admissions—at times with numerical targets—to compensate for patterns of bias against women and racial minorities. Without adequate news coverage of how those patterns persist in the present, such compensatory programs are liable to seem nonsensical.

Ironically, part of the problem is due to the inadequacy of affirmative action inside the media business itself. While amounting to fully one quarter of the U.S. population, racial minorities account for only 7.7 percent of newsroom supervisors at the nation's newspapers. The situation is commonly worse elsewhere in the media industry.

The fact is that journalists who've benefited from affirmative action usually have little power. Managers, editors, senior reporters and top pundits—and, most importantly, their bosses— are still, overwhelmingly, white males.

It often seems that white commentators are more opposed to *criticism* of racism than to racism itself.

Here's what *Time* magazine staffer Lance Morrow wrote three months ago [Dec. 5, 1994] in a column denouncing affirmative action: "If I were something like the Pope of black America and had the moral authority to make such suggestions, I would propose that no African-American use the terms racism or racist." It was a revealing fantasy for a white journalist who has not shrunk from applying the term racism to black bigotry against whites.

"Today, though we live in a world...that is increasingly multicultural, much of the conventional journalism remains fixated on the lives of the white and the wealthy," notes *Newsweek* contributing editor Ellis Cose. He adds that "achieving better and more balanced journalism ultimately depends on having journalists who are wise enough and varied enough to see the world in its true complexity."

In 1978, the American Society of Newspaper Editors launched a campaign for—in effect—affirmative action. Despite strides that have been made, at last count only 10.5 percent of newspaper journalists are racial minorities, less than half of the proportion in the overall population. Without affirmative action, the figures surely would be even bleaker.

And, as Cose points out, "even if newspapers can manage to achieve demographic parity with the general population"—a goal that remains distant—"that alone will not guarantee a more honest and representative brand of reporting. The problem lies as much in our attitudes as in our statistics."

Calls for discarding affirmative action in favor of "color-blind" policies are actually urgings that we be blind to history—and to current realities of unequal opportunity. If news media were doing a better job, the myth that discrimination against minorities is just a thing of the past would be far less prevalent.

The persistence of racial bias is not difficult to reveal. ABC's *PrimeTime Live* once used hidden cameras to show what happens all too often when equally qualified blacks and whites apply for the same jobs or apartment rentals; the TV program documented recurring discrimination against African-Americans. (A follow-up program also demonstrated widespread bias against female applicants.)

Let's be clear: Hostility toward affirmative action often runs parallel with tacit belief in white superiority. After all, if affirmative action is unnecessary—if the effects of racism are just in the past—then how else can we explain the low number of blacks and other racial minorities in a wide range of professions today?

As an antidote to popular prejudices, the public would benefit from more media attention to the work of Stephen Jay Gould, the eminent scientist who debunked racial quantifications of intelligence in his classic book *The Mismeasure of Man*.

More recently, in the February [1995] issue of *Natural History* magazine, Gould traces the continuity of what he calls "academic racism," spanning from the 1850s to the present day. His essay is titled "Ghosts of Bell Curves Past."

Gould, a professor of biology and the history of science at Harvard University, refutes key myths about intelligence—myths that serve as ammunition for opponents of programs for racial equality.

- Myth #1: "The wonderfully multifarious and multidimensional set of human attributes that we call intelligence" can be boiled down to one gauge of "general intellectual capacity."

- Myth #2: The "amount" of someone's intelligence "must be abstractable as a single number (usually called IQ)," and this number can rank people's intelligence.

- Myth #3: This single IQ number measures largely inherited capabilities.

- Myth #4: "A person's IQ score must be stable and permanent—subject to little change (only minor and temporary tinkering) by any program of social and educational intervention."

Gould's essay demolishes each of these myths. Along the way, he points out that "if any of these assumptions fails, the entire argument and associated political agenda goes belly-up." And he shows that foes of egalitarian social programs have long tried to popularize such misconceptions as a way of rationalizing extreme inequities—and perpetuating them.

The battle over affirmative action is part of a much larger question: *Should we acknowledge our shared humanity by striving to nurture all people to fulfill their potentials?* As a scientist, Gould finds an affirmative answer in the field of evolutionary biology—which, he concludes, "has discovered the sources of human unity in minimal genetic distances among our races and in the geological yesterday of our common origin."

March 1, 1995

Who does what?

*Women represent 51.2 percent of the U.S. adult population,
blacks 12.4 percent and Hispanics 9.5 percent.*

Share of positions held by:	Women	Blacks	Hispanics
Doctors	22.3%	4.2%	5.2%
Nurses	93.8%	9.3%	2.9%
Teachers (COLLEGES, UNIVERSITIES)	42.5%	5.0%	2.9%
All other teachers	74.9%	8.9%	4.3%
Engineers	8.3%	3.7%	3.3%
Lawyers	24.6%	3.3%	3.1%
Architects	16.8%	1.4%	3.7%
Natural scientists	31.0%	3.6%	1.6%
Clergy	11.1%	8.7%	3.2%
Construction trades	2.2%	6.5%	11.4%
Firefighters	2.1%	9.1%	5.4%
Librarians	84.1%	10.5%	3.7%

USN&WR—Basic data: U.S. Dept. of Labor

The loud cover of *U.S. News* is contradicted by a chart inside showing
that white men continue to dominate key professions and skilled crafts.

Clarence Thomas:
Affirmative Action Success Story

There is something unseemly about a guy who's just built a house on the beach and is now leading the charge to stop all further beach-front construction.

Or a recent immigrant who climbs the soapbox to call for a halt to further immigration.

Or a beneficiary of affirmative-action programs who climbs the ladder of success by attacking affirmative action.

That kind of unseemliness was demonstrated this month [June1995] by Justice Clarence Thomas. But few reporters took note—even though it should be the media's job to spotlight hypocrisy.

Thomas cast the deciding vote in the Supreme Court's 5-to-4 decision narrowing federal affirmative-action programs. But Thomas went beyond even fellow conservatives on the bench—he argued for an immediate end to affirmative action.

There's an obvious contradiction here: Clarence Thomas benefited enormously from the kind of affirmative-action programs he now seeks to kill.

Indeed, Thomas' rise from his dirt-poor upbringing in rural Georgia into an elite Ivy League law school is an affirmative-action success story. But don't take our word for it. Take his.

In a November 1983 speech to his staff at the federal Equal Employment Opportunities Commission, Thomas called affirmative action "critical to minorities and women in this society."

Then his remarks got personal: "But for them [affirmative-action laws], God only knows where I would be today. These laws and their proper application are all that stand between the first 17 years of my life and the second 17 years."

As an undergraduate at Holy Cross College, Thomas received a scholarship set aside for racial minorities. He was admitted to Yale Law School in 1971 as part of an aggressive (and successful) affirmative-action program with a clear goal: 10 percent minority enrollment. Yale offered him generous financial aid.

Affirmative action can't guarantee success, but it can open doors previously closed to women or people of color. The rest is up to those who walk through the doors.

By all accounts, Thomas was a hard worker who studied long hours. But his place at Yale Law School—his key to later success—was opened by a race-conscious admissions program, the kind he is now intent on outlawing.

After this month's Supreme Court decision, few news outlets explored the sharp contrast between Clarence Thomas' obsession with destroying affirmative action and his own personal history. If mainstream journalists shed light on programs like the one at Yale—which helped admit a young man raised in a shack without running water—these policies might well be popular.

One wonders what Thomas believes about his past. Maybe he prefers the fairy-tale account provided by Rush Limbaugh, whose talk show he listens to each day: "Clarence Thomas escaped the bonds of poverty by methods other than those prescribed by these civil-rights organizations. He has succeeded by relying on himself, rather than prostituting himself into the dependency cycle."

The truth is that Thomas owes thanks to the civil-rights movement—whose decades of lawsuits, protests and lobbying removed barriers for individuals like Thomas. Yet, he seems to relish his role as one of the movement's main enemies.

Since the early 1980s, Thomas' career soared thanks to a perverse form of racial preference. It was his race, as Thomas has admitted, that got him two civil-rights posts in the Reagan White House; the jobs came because he opposed the civil-rights movement. So did his boss, President Reagan, whose opposition dated back to the years of Martin Luther King Jr.

President Bush—who, like Reagan, had opposed the landmark 1964 Civil Rights Act—later chose Thomas to fill the Supreme Court seat of civil-rights stalwart Thurgood Marshall, the only other African-American to sit on the highest court.

In his recent Supreme Court opinion blasting affirmative action, Justice Thomas went soft on white racist lawmakers by saying he could find no moral difference between "laws designed to subjugate a race" and laws that benefit a race "in order to foster some current notion of equality."

Thomas went on to complain that affirmative-action programs stigmatize the beneficiaries—an argument not raised by the plaintiff in the case, a white building contractor who says he unfairly lost federal work to a Latino-owned business.

Responding to Thomas, Justice John Paul Stevens pointed out that if beneficiaries of affirmative action feel stigmatized, they can simply "opt out of the program."

It's worth considering. If Justice Thomas feels traumatized or stigmatized for having benefited from affirmative action, he could give back his law diploma.

Such a move would be absurd—since Thomas earned his degree by studying hard and passing all required exams.

Even more absurd, though, is Thomas' current mania for closing doors—for others—that the civil-rights movement helped open for him.

June 21, 1995

USA Today
Turns Away from Diversity

For a long time, *USA Today* has deserved credit for venturing beyond the usual limits of commentary. One big reason: Since the late 1980s, a weekly column by Barbara Reynolds kept challenging readers to consider views rarely seen or heard in mass media.

No more. This month [July 1996], "the nation's newspaper" fired her.

Reynolds was not just an extraordinary columnist at *USA Today*. She was also the only African-American on the newspaper's 11-member editorial board. In her column—and in the board's deliberations—she did not settle for token status. Reynolds insisted on being a voice for people who routinely go unheard.

Each Friday, next to her picture, that voice rose from newsprint and soared above the facile media choir. Singing out against inequity and injustice, Reynolds advocated for the poor and the powerless. She urged that Americans summon the determination to make room at the inn for everyone.

In her farewell column on July 12, Reynolds wrote that "this is not the time for muted voices." An ordained Christian minister, she pledged to continue her efforts "to help bring harmony in an age of division when churches are burning, affirmative action is under siege and forces ranging from a conservative court to angry white militias threaten to strip people of color of their dignity and rights."

Why was she fired?

USA Today's editorial-page editor, Karen Jurgensen, gave us the official story: "We made a decision that we weren't going to have any more in-house columnists on the editorial and op-ed pages."

And how many such columnists did *USA Today* have?

"Barbara was the only one," Jurgensen acknowledged. Despite denials from management, the ousting of Barbara Reynolds was clearly a political move. "The direction of the paper is becoming more conservative, and Barbara did not fit in," a former *USA Today* reporter told us. "The bottom line is the bottom line at the paper."

With top managers eager to attract more big-ticket advertisers, recent *USA Today* directives have pushed employees to orient the paper toward a target readership of affluent travelers, symbolized by a white male driving a plush Lexus. During the past two years, the paper has rid itself of a number of journalists disinclined to march to such a beat.

Self-described as "an African-American, a progressive, a feminist and a seminarian," Reynolds offered colleagues and readers a passionate mix of identity, commitment and faith. Her firing was part of a narrow-minded housecleaning at the only general-interest newspaper that reaches millions of Americans nationwide.

Soon after *USA Today*'s launch in 1982, the paper won plaudits from the National Association of Black Journalists for promoting diversity in its staff and on its pages. But during the 1990s, *USA Today* has been reversing course—drastically. According to an NABJ statement, last fall "a newsroom committee formed to monitor and promote diversity was so disillusioned it disbanded itself."

The situation has now worsened with the removal of "the only African-American remaining to offer opinions as the editorial board met each morning," the NABJ observes. Meanwhile, "African-American opinion writers can't help but interpret this move as meaning that unless one toes the line in these conservative political times, we too are subject to being fired or harassed."

As it happens, Barbara Reynolds chairs the Women's Task Force of the National Association of Black Journalists. When 2,000 members of the NABJ meet for its annual convention next month, they'll have a lot to discuss.

What *USA Today* has done is not merely a professional matter. The underlying issues should concern all Americans who care about news media and democracy. Often, the voices that are most difficult to hear are the ones we most need to consider. In the words of poet Audre Lorde, "It is not difference which immobilizes us most but silence."

July 17, 1996

the editorial ——
nce as a journalist and

By Barbara Reynolds

—gulations that worked to
care profe——

ATION'S NEWSPAPER

USA DAY

I must say goodbye to a labor of love

Goodbye. In all of my 450 columns, some 250,000 words, this is one word I had hoped I'd never use. But this column is my last.
— USA TODAY for allo—— —e to pour my e—— — —
—nto "

Part VIII
Media Haves
and Have-Nots

Some people in our society get lavish media attention. Celebrities, no matter how boring, are big news. But mass media tell us little about a broad range of un-moneyed, real-life heros. As for certain groups, like Arab-Americans and Muslims, they're prone to get caught in a huge media spotlight—one often colored by prejudice.

Knee-Jerk Coverage
of Oklahoma Bombing
Should Not Be Forgotten

So much has happened since the horrendous bombing in Oklahoma that the initial media coverage may already seem like a distant memory. But one person who will never forget is Saher Al-Saidi, a refugee from Iraq, living in Oklahoma City.

The morning after the explosion—following nearly 24 hours of knee-jerk news coverage that linked the terrorism to Muslims and Arabs—vigilantes shattered the windows of her home with stones. Not quite seven months pregnant, she began experiencing abdominal pain and internal bleeding; her baby was stillborn.

Across the country, many other Muslims and Arab-Americans were harassed and threatened.

Hours after the bomb went off, *CBS Evening News* featured Steven Emerson, a ubiquitous "terrorism expert," who eagerly presented his biases as objective analysis: "This was done with the intent to inflict as many casualties as possible. That is a Middle Eastern trait."

In the wake of the bombing, media outlets rounded up the stock "terrorism experts" and paraded them across TV screens and front pages. For nearly two days, we heard from touted experts whose utter lack of evidence was masked by bold assertions about a foreign menace threatening America's heartland.

On the CNBC cable-TV network, Cal Thomas' show featured an expert warning of illegal immigrants "coming in to destroy our democracy."

Columnist Georgie Ann Geyer asserted that the bombing "has every single earmark of the Islamic car-bombers of the Middle East." Geyer relied on Emerson's claim that the Oklahoma City area is "one of the centers for Islamic radicalism outside the Middle East."

A front-page *Christian Science Monitor* article asked: "Who would have thought that terrorism would reach so far into the nation's heartland?" Answers came from a bevy of think tank experts who showed no inkling that terror might originate from *inside* "the nation's heartland."

In a *Newsday* column, self-styled terrorism expert Jeff Kamen wrote of a large "Islamic fundamentalist" community in Oklahoma City and imputed a "massive failure" to the federal government for not preventing the attack given that "so much was known about potential terrorists in the area."

U.S. military commandoes should "shoot them [terrorists] now, before they get us," wrote Kamen. Now that he has a clue about who was behind the bombing, would he advocate sending Navy Seals to shoot ultra-rightists in rural America?

The *New York Times* speculated in its first day of reporting on why terrorists would have struck in Oklahoma City: "Some Middle Eastern groups have held meetings there, and the city is home to at least three mosques."

Is the presence of houses of worship now grounds for suspecting a terrorist threat?

What is haunting about the performance of these mainstream, "quality" news outlets is that they exhibited the paranoia and xenophobia—albeit in milder doses—that one hears from right-wing militia groups: fear of foreigners, belief in dark conspiracies beyond our nation's control.

Most mainstream journalists were caught flat-footed by the militia story. Perhaps that's why they believe—mistakenly, in our view—that federal agencies need new powers of infiltration in order to monitor and prosecute criminal elements among the extremists.

For two years, "patriot" militias have grown steadily—as have efforts by neo-Nazis and other white supremacists to join and take over the militias. But heightened police powers aren't needed to track these trends.

Human rights groups and independent journalists have been monitoring these militias from the beginning. It can be as easy as cruising the Internet. Or monitoring short-wave radio. Or turning on AM talk radio.

Two months ago, we wrote a column exposing the supportive role played by certain talk-radio hosts for the militia movement. We weren't privy to any covert channels of information—we simply examined what was happening on the air waves.

For example, we published the remarks of Colorado Springs talk host Chuck Baker, whose program last summer provided a friendly forum for extremist militia strategies, including calls for an armed march on Washington.

We also reported on G. Gordon Liddy's instructions to militia groups—offered last August on his nationally syndicated radio talk show—about how to kill agents of the federal Bureau of Alcohol, Tobacco and Firearms: "Head shots. Head shots."

Since the Oklahoma bombing, Liddy has amended his instructions—"shoot to the groin area"—while telling listeners how to build a home-made bomb.

Broadcasting from New York, hate-radio pioneer Bob Grant has been a magnet for callers from neo-Nazi and white supremacist groups—who have used Grant's show to publicize their propaganda and phone numbers.

The day after the Oklahoma bombing, Grant was in usual form: declaring that Islam is a "violent" religion, that Muslims were behind the detonation—and expressing his desire to shoot a caller who warned of rushing to judgment.

Instead of engaging in dangerous speculation, the media's "terrorism experts" might do better to monitor extremists—by flipping on the AM radio dial.

And besides scrutinizing governments that sponsor international terrorism, they might examine media companies that promote domestic extremism.

April 26, 1995

Hidden Costs
of America's Celebrity Obsession

Anyone who shops at a supermarket ends up in "celebrity alley"—a checkout lane that's lined with magazines fixated on the famous. In America, celebrities take up a lot of space—on newsstands, coffee tables and TV screens, and in our minds.

More than 20 years have passed since *People* magazine first appeared. Today, it's one of many slick, fame-crazed periodicals with sales in the millions. Meanwhile, television is so transfixed with celebrities that news programs often resemble "tabloid TV."

There's nothing wrong with keeping track of events in the lives of celebrities. Occasional diversion is one thing—but perpetual distraction is another.

Reverence for celebrities is the flip side of tacit contempt for "average" people. It can be an insidious process: As we focus on the famous, other people fade into our peripheral vision. By an unspoken and unconscious logic, the world becomes populated with a few somebodies and a glut of near-nobodies.

The slippery slope of fame-fixation puts our sense of human proportion on the skids. The danger is that when celebrities matter more, the rest of us matter less.

With wealth and fame going hand-in-hand, the modern equivalent of the golden calf occupies center stage. And, in practice, worship of the rich has a way of accompanying denigration of the poor. If having plenty of money makes one person important, then having no money makes another person unimportant.

For media conglomerates like Time Warner—which owns *People* and has launched still another glossy magazine, *In Style*—the point is to post big profits. Along the way, it's just fine if the products encourage us to look down our noses at "ordinary" people while gazing up the social ladder for inspiration.

The April [1996] issue of *In Style* is thick with 154 pages of sumptuous photo spreads and ads offering vicarious thrills. The cover features such stories as "Sexy Celebrity Bedrooms" and "Hollywood's Hottest: Dresses, Hairdos and Parties."

Yet, truth be told, beyond their performances and public-relations glitz, most celebs aren't all that interesting. On television, when a renowned actor or singer chats with Jay Leno or David Letterman, frequently the conversation is lame. Without a script, many celebrities have little to say and take a long time saying it.

While celebrity-mania runs amuck, "common" people are likely to be ignored or disparaged. Thinking back on a journalistic career spanning several decades, Ben Bagdikian said recently, "it always put my teeth on edge when I would hear certain kinds of academics or intellectuals or others talk about 'the great unwashed.'"

Bagdikian, a former high-ranking editor at the *Washington Post*, told us that he loathed portrayals of working-class Americans "as one great homogenized body of people who aren't very smart and who are sort of like cattle." So-called average men and women "are real people, and they have all the attributes of any human beings. Some of them are rotten and some of them are heroes, and most of them are interesting, complex beings."

On a daily basis, however, we get scant illumination of the human complexities of the unrich and unfamous. While the spotlight remains on the glamorous and the powerful, common courage gets only a faint glimmer of the attention it deserves.

Imagine standing in a checkout line and seeing magazine stands filled with stories about individuals who've been doing laudable things routinely—caring for an elderly parent or struggling to raise children with meager resources or walking a lonely picket line in defense of the right to decent employment.

The truth is that our country is teeming with heroes, never to be famous, quietly striving to live with kindness, dignity and integrity. They don't step out of limousines; they won't ever be on a "best dressed list" or become familiar images on national television.

Most people we know are light years away from celebrity status. Even the most fleeting fame will never be theirs. And it's all too easy for us to forget, day to day, just how admirable and inspiring they can be.

April 3, 1996

USA:
The Union-busting States of America?

If you doubt that the freedom to voluntarily join a labor union is a basic human right, think back about a dozen years.

That's when President Reagan waxed eloquent about the right of workers in Poland to form unions. American pundits and editorial writers loudly hailed the right of Polish workers to join the Solidarity union.

But that was then.

Today, most U.S. media are quiet about another country where the right to organize unions has virtually disappeared. It's a country where workers are often spied on, threatened or fired when they try to launch unions. It's a country known as the United States of America—or perhaps that should be "the Union-busting States of America."

On Labor Day weekend, media outlets tend to serve up parades and platitudes about the value of labor. You don't hear much outrage about American workers losing the right to form unions.

It's a nationwide story easy to document through first-hand accounts—the kind of people-oriented news that media, especially TV, often seem to love. Yet you've probably never heard of:

- *Connie McMillan, a psychiatric nurse in Alabama*. Last January [1995], she hosted a private meeting in her living room where 13 nurses signed union cards. Two days later, the hospital fired 10 of them. "It's our right to belong to a union," said McMillan. "I can't believe this is happening."

- *Lew Hubble, a K-Mart warehouseman in Illinois*. He and some colleagues convinced a majority of their co-workers to vote to form a union. But at great cost: Spies hired by K-Mart spent months reporting not only on their union activities, but also intimate details of their personal and family lives.

"The first union meeting I ever went to I went with the undercover investigator, the spy, and I didn't know what he was," said Hubble, a 30-year K-Mart employee. "It's the kind of thing you'd expect in a Communist country.... You don't expect this in the United States."

- *Betty Dumas, a pipefitter at Louisiana's Avondale shipyards.* Uniting across racial lines in 1993, shipyard workers voted to form a union by a 500-vote margin. Years later, they have no union—because Avondale is contesting the election and simply refuses to recognize the union. Workers claim they've been threatened, harassed and fired for supporting the union.

  "When you vote for president, once he's voted in, he's given a seat," says Dumas, who once saw a co-worker crushed to death by a two-ton piece of steel. "Why is it taking so long for the union to come in?" Seven Avondale workers have died in shipyard accidents in the last three years.

  Avondale pay-stubs once conveyed a chilling message: "The squeaking wheel doesn't always get the grease. Sometimes it gets replaced."

- *Martin Levitt, a former corporate consultant and author of "Confessions of a Union Buster."* For 20 years, he provided the brain, brawn and payoffs to "independent" committees of workers willing to lead the fight against formation of a union. "The only way to bust a union," says Levitt, "is to lie, distort, manipulate, threaten and always, always attack."

- *Kara Holman, a Louisville nurse.* Because of her union activity at the Audubon hospital, she and another nurse assert they were "blacklisted" from other employment. According to the testimony of a former Audubon manager, the hospital's human resources director warned a second hospital that the nurses were "union red-hots" and that "you probably don't want them working for you."

Pipefitter Betty Dumas

Warehouseman Lew Hubble

- *Florence Hill, a 60-year-old textile worker in Georgia.* She testified at a federal hearing last year that Highland Yarn Mills repeatedly harassed her and her husband during a union election campaign. "When I'd go to the bathroom, the supervisor would follow me," Hill stated under oath. "And then pornographic pictures, things I had never dreamed of before, were placed in my drawers—and notes placed all over the mill insinuating that I was having an affair with another man."

    Recalled Hill, nearly in tears: "The stress got so bad that I had a heart attack."

These personal stories of union-busting are so vivid that it's remarkable how rarely they're explored in national media. Thankfully, all these accounts and more are presented in an exceptional TV documentary, *Ties That Bind*, which aired this Labor Day weekend [1995] on over 100 PBS stations.

It is illegal—in theory at least—for companies to harass or fire workers for union activity, or to refuse to recognize a union supported by a majority of the workers. The hard-fought right to form unions was established in the 1930s during the New Deal and the tumultuous battles for industrial unionism.

But law-breaking is now common in American work places, and corporations that engage in chronic union-busting activities are often just slapped on the wrist by the National Labor Relations Board or the courts.

It's telling that the same corporate interests lobbying successfully in Washington to undo decades of consumer, environmental and safety regulations don't want any changes at all in labor law or enforcement.

In *Ties That Bind*—a documentary from the producers of the public TV series *We Do The Work*—spokespersons for employers and the U.S. Chamber of Commerce insist that "labor law" works just fine and that no reform is needed.

Workplace issues could be dramatically explored on television, but even PBS is wary. *Ties That Bind* launches the sixth season of *We Do The Work*, the unique series that has progressed without support from PBS at the national level, and without a penny from the Corporation for Public Broadcasting.

Washington PBS bureaucrats show little interest in programs that address the job-related concerns of the vast majority of Americans who work for a salary or wage. But if you're among the small minority of Americans who actively invest on Wall Street, PBS stations offer various regular programs for your viewing pleasure.

In the 1980s, when Lech Walesa led Poland's Solidarity union against a corrupt Communist regime that outlawed independent unions, he was canonized by U.S. news media.

Today, many American workers are fighting for the democratic right to organize unions. Yet there's little enthusiasm in mainstream media for these American heroes.

[In 1996, *We Do The Work* went on hiatus as a weekly series—partly for lack of support from national public TV officials.]

August 30, 1995

Silencing Prisoners
Is a Crime Against Journalism

Few people are talked about more—and heard from less—than prisoners.

Rarely do we turn on a television or pick up a newspaper and learn what prisoners have to say. Without direct communication, they don't seem very real to us as human beings. As a result, it's much easier for us to demand ever-harsher prison terms.

Sometimes, a convict isn't even guilty. Until last month, George Perchea was among the more than 1 million Americans behind bars. But—after two years inside a Philadelphia jail for a drug conviction—he went free in late July [1995]. A judge belatedly found that Perchea had been nailed by testimony of police who'd planted contraband on innocent people.

"The City of Brotherly Love" seems to be rife with serious misconduct by police. Another innocent prisoner, on death row for four years, was able to avoid lethal injection only because of revelations that Philadelphia police had committed perjury in order to frame him.

The sentence of another man, Mumia Abu-Jamal, may soon become irreversible.

This summer [1995], a flickering national media spotlight has fallen on Pennsylvania's death row. Abu-Jamal—an African-American advocate of radical change who has worked as an award-winning radio journalist—is scheduled to be executed in mid-August.

In a lengthy *New York Times* op-ed article [July 14, 1995], novelist E.L. Doctorow presented reasons to doubt that Abu-Jamal is guilty of murdering a police officer—the criminal conviction that put him on death row.

Yet, for a long time—despite years of work by activists pressing his case—national media virtually ignored Abu-Jamal.

The Fraternal Order of Police in Philadelphia has fought for the "principle" of silencing prisoners like Abu-Jamal. This spring, the group waged a fierce campaign to prevent publication of his new book, *Live From Death Row*. Fortunately, the publisher, Addison-Wesley, proved to have more backbone than National Public Radio.

In May 1994, NPR announced plans to air a series of Abu-Jamal's already-recorded commentaries about crime and prison life. But when Philadelphia police objected, NPR management caved in—and *All Things Considered* listeners didn't hear a word from Abu-Jamal.

Since late last year, the prison system has rejected requests from scores of journalists to interview Mumia Abu-Jamal. Several TV networks meekly accepted the rejections and then canceled plans for stories.

But journalistic groups recently took action. Last month, the Society of Professional Journalists and five other national organizations, representing reporters and editors, urged a federal court to stand up for the First Amendment in Abu-Jamal's case.

The right of prisoners to be heard—and of the public to hear them—seems to be quite perishable in the United States. The pattern is clear: When prison authorities don't like the content of what a prisoner has to say, they try to nullify the First Amendment.

On rare occasions, media outlets resist such interference.

Much good resulted from the *San Francisco Chronicle*'s decision to go to court in 1988 on behalf of a 48-year-old prisoner. By then, Dannie Martin had been writing articles for that newspaper for two years.

Trouble arose only when the *Chronicle* published a piece by Martin that criticized the Lompoc, California, federal prison administration for its "gulag mentality." The warden retaliated—ordering Martin thrown into solitary confinement and then transferred to a prison in Phoenix.

"They wanted to put chains and shackles on my voice," Martin said later. He added: "I committed bank robbery and they put me in prison, and that was right. Then I committed journalism and they put me in the hole. And that was wrong."

Dannie Martin and his editor at the *Chronicle*, Peter Sussman, persevered with their path-breaking efforts. Between 1986 and 1991, the *Chronicle* published more than 50 of Martin's eloquent articles about life behind prison walls.

With poignant humor and insight, Martin wrote about realities that are routinely fenced off from people on the outside. (His articles, combined with Sussman's narrative, appear in the book *Committing Journalism*, now out in paperback.)

When his writings became a courtroom issue, Martin testified: "Letters I got from people outside made me realize to what extent they don't have any idea what's in a criminal's mind. They see a guy on TV bust someone's head, and he's off the picture.... He doesn't have a wife and family. He's just a thug. They see him for a minute, and he's gone. And they wind up with a stereotype of what a criminal is, and it's wrong."

Sussman recalls that "prison officials would later argue that convict writing in the news media under a byline is dangerous to security because of its effects on other prisoners"— but officials "seemed primarily concerned about what outsiders were able to learn of the internal workings of the prison."

For a few years, the *Chronicle*'s battle with prison authorities dragged through federal courts, which ultimately ruled the matter moot when Martin was released from prison in 1991. As things now stand, laments Sussman, "any future prison writers— or their publishers—will have to go through a similar costly and uncertain crusade before federal convicts gain the unambiguous right to publish anything more than a letter to the editor in the news media."

Supporters of the harshest measures against prisoners— including the death penalty—tend to be the most opposed to letting them be heard in news media. But Sussman, who is among the nation's most experienced editors on prison issues, sees things differently.

"In the United States today, one of journalism's most urgent callings is to explore the roots of our out-of-control crime problems," Sussman says. "We cannot hope to solve those crippling problems without understanding them from all perspectives—perpetrator as well as victim, police officer, prison guard, warden, judge, government policymaker, and academic expert. Of those perspectives, perhaps the least understood and least available is that of the criminal."

Sussman notes that abuses "are bound to flourish in closed, authoritarian institutions" such as prisons. Journalism has a responsibility to intrude into places that rarely see the light of day.

"In his dispatches from prison, Dannie did not exonerate his fellow prisoners," Sussman points out. "But he gave them back their names and personalities and families and the same vulnerable emotions we all have. He restored their human complexity. That may be the first step out of our quagmire of crime and punishment."

August 2, 1995

A Media Tale of Two Bombs

"A lie can go halfway around the world before the truth even gets its boots on," Mark Twain once said. Sometimes, accurate information is able to catch up and prevail. But too often, we're kept in the dark while truth fumbles with its laces.

You remember Richard Jewell—the Atlanta security guard who found a bomb just before it exploded during the Olympics in July [1996]. News media soon proclaimed that Jewell was the FBI's prime suspect. Some outlets seemed bent on convicting him.

It wasn't until October that federal authorities admitted they'd been wrong. When that happened, the mass media provided Jewell with some sympathetic coverage. Naturally, after months of notoriety, he wanted the media to set the record straight.

Judi Bari has a similar wish. But she's still waiting for corrective action from news outlets that took a wild FBI smear and plastered it on America's front pages more than six years ago.

Apparently, when it comes to defaming outside-the-system environmental activists, being the FBI—or mainstream media—means never having to say you're sorry.

Bari was driving down an Oakland, Calif. street when a bomb exploded under her shortly before noon on May 24, 1990. Her companion, fellow Earth First! activist Darryl Cherney, suffered minor injuries. But shrapnel tore into Bari's body, shattering her pelvis and decimating vital organs.

Two days later, as Bari fought for her life in a hospital bed, a front-page *New York Times* article reported that she and Cherney—"two leaders of a radical environmental group"—had been "charged with possession and transportation of an explosive device."

Prodded by the FBI, which was hostile toward Earth First!, the Oakland police claimed to have solved the crime with lightning speed. The *Times* article spotlighted a police lieutenant who "said the authorities believed that the bomb had been placed in the car by its occupants and that it had detonated accidentally." The officer added ominously: "We're making the assumption that if the bomb was built, it was meant to be used."

Nationwide, this was very hot news, evoking images of bomb-toting eco-fanatics. But the story quickly unraveled.

Eager to depict the bombing's victims as its perpetrators, police announced that the bomb must have been plainly visible on the back-seat floorboard. Actually, clear evidence—confirmed by an expert FBI examiner—showed that the bomb had been concealed under the driver's seat. What's more, the explosive device was designed to detonate from the motion of a moving vehicle.

Before the bomb went off in her car, Bari had received death threats because of her prominent work to save ancient redwood forests. She kept calling for nonviolent direct action to block rapacious timber interests.

After arresting the two activists with great fanfare, police lacked any evidence against Bari and Cherney. Charges were quietly dropped—and national media yawned at the turnaround. The hot story had cooled, so why dwell on it?

If Bari and Cherney had been high-paid lobbyists instead of grass-roots activists, the FBI and major media would not have created an image of them as likely mad bombers. It's easier to smear people who wear jeans and defend old-growth forests instead of plying their trade in three-piece suits on Capitol Hill.

For several years now, Judi Bari has been working hard on a lawsuit against the police and the FBI. She and Darryl Cherney want public acknowledgment that there was an official campaign to neutralize Earth First! efforts. "The FBI knowingly lied about the evidence in order to bring about our arrest," Bari says. And news media were much more interested in spreading the lies than correcting them.

The wheels of litigation grind slow—especially when the government is doing all it can to put sand in the gears. Justice may never reach the court docket or the mass media.

Meanwhile, the truth about the bombing that nearly killed Judi Bari is still struggling to get its boots on.

[Bari died of breast cancer in March 1997 at the age of 47.]

November 27, 1996

Prejudice That Kills:
The Toll in AIDS

Not long ago, driving on an interstate highway, we were listening to the radio when a man on a request line asked that a love song be dedicated to "Tony."

The disc jockey shot back: "I hope that's 'Toni' with an 'i.'"

The man on the phone quickly assured the DJ that his loved one was indeed female.

Such talk on the airwaves might seem inconsequential. It's not. The reinforcement of timeworn prejudices has deadly results.

"Stigma and discrimination are the enemies of public health," says Dr. Jonathan Mann, director of the International AIDS Center at Harvard University. He has written the preface to an important new report —"The Impact of Homophobia and Other Social Biases on AIDS"—released by the Public Media Center based in San Francisco.

Though media coverage has slacked off during the last several years, the AIDS crisis has not. On the contrary: Among Americans between the ages of 24 and 44, AIDS is now the leading cause of death. Worldwide, by the end of 1995, more than 5 million people had died from the disease.

"Our nation is suffering in the midst of an unprecedented public health emergency in which more than a million Americans may be diagnosed with AIDS by the year 2000—nearly one out of every 250 Americans," the report notes.

"Yet, as a nation, we continue to work in the dark, without fully implementing a national AIDS plan, without a concerted national commitment to conquering the AIDS crisis and without sufficient public or private resources to deal with the issue."

Ask yourself: If, 15 years ago, a cross-section of the American people had become infected with AIDS via heterosexual intercourse, would the federal government have been so slow to respond? And would anti-AIDS endeavors still be so low on the agendas of elected officials and mass media?

In the early 1980s, AIDS became known as a disease afflicting gay men. Since then, AIDS has spread widely, hitting the poor especially hard. Boosted by intravenous drug use, the illness is killing large numbers of blacks and Latinos.

"Irrational prejudices like homophobia have obstructed public health efforts that prevent the spread of AIDS," the Public Media Center points out. The stigma attached to AIDS is a "social pathology that distorts public policy, fuels infection and subverts AIDS care."

These days, it's true that we're likely to see quite a few laudable, empathetic news stories about people with AIDS. We're also apt to see in-depth scientific articles about AIDS research in the mainstream press.

But an AIDS *crisis*, with a terribly urgent need for much more effective countermeasures? Judging from routine media coverage, such a crisis does not exist.

The nation's persisting failure to confront the AIDS epidemic is directly linked to anti-gay prejudices, as the new report makes clear:

- "Despite the fact that numerous 'risk groups' have been associated with HIV/AIDS, the disease has maintained its greatest hold on the public imagination in terms of its connection to gay and bisexual men....This perception coincides with an underlying and prevalent homophobia."

- The obstacles to effectively mobilizing against AIDS are especially difficult "because homophobia has never been addressed through an open, public dialogue, and because a social consensus condemning homophobia has never been formed."

- Anti-gay prejudices, combined with a common view of AIDS as a gay disease, "continue to hamper our efforts to address this as a health crisis not only for gay and bisexual men but for women, for people of color, for intravenous drug users and for other populations."

The report urges Americans to "address homophobia as an independent moral issue involving the goals of fairness, human dignity and the promotion of social tolerance and understanding."

Clearly, wide implementation of preventive measures will be necessary to stop the AIDS epidemic. Even now, however, news media provide sparse information.

If only the major media outlets were as good at informing the public about AIDS prevention as they are at informing us about superficial events in the lives of Hollywood celebrities.

Halting the spread of AIDS will require "continual" and "pervasive" messages encouraging protective behavior, the Public Media Center report concludes. AIDS is an "indiscriminate killer that we allow to thrive only as a result of our own unconfronted prejudices, fears and ambivalence."

By confronting our own prejudices, we can turn away from ambivalence — and move toward determination to end the AIDS crisis.

January 17, 1996

Part IX
Media Idols and Pariahs

Some public figures and journalists in our country are treated as media icons—their faults overlooked, their remarks ever-amplified and rarely challenged. Others, who bring special wisdom or wit to American life, are often locked out of mainstream discourse. Who is in which category says much about media bias.

"Powellmania":
Don't Believe the Hype

After years of glowing coverage and avid speculation about his political future, it's time for news media to start asking tough questions about Colin Powell.

Newsweek has called Gen. Powell "the most respected figure in American public life." Last month [August 1995], *Time* magazine described him as "the Persian Gulf War hero who exudes strength, common sense and human values like no one else on the scene."

But such accolades were mere warm-ups for the Powellmania that's just beginning.

Release of the retired general's autobiography is set to tip over a huge row of PR dominos this fall. With a *Time* cover story featuring book excerpts and network TV interviews kicking off a whirlwind 25-city tour, Powell's media star is likely to rise into the political heavens.

Amid all the hoopla about the first black American to become a four-star Army general and chairman of the Joint Chiefs of Staff, the media spin presents Powell as a pillar of integrity who could transform American politics in 1996.

"The polls show he could win the presidency," *Time* declared recently. "But is he bold enough to go for the top job and take on the political establishment?"

Here's a better question: What are the odds that a Powell campaign would really "take on the political establishment" when his career was *made possible by* the political establishment?

And who would fund a Powell-for-president campaign? Answer: The establishment.

A "former Pentagon official who now works in corporate America" told *Time*: "I could raise $50 million in one month just from the CEOs I know." When he spoke to the American Bar Association a few weeks ago, Powell pocketed a check for

$60,000— a fee donated by a consumer-finance firm. Such funding is hardly from upset-the-apple-cart sources.

While many news outlets replay endless variations of "This is your life, Colin Powell," they have been slow to examine certain aspects of his record. Here's a sampling:

- In December 1968, as an Army major assigned to the Americal Division headquarters in Vietnam, Powell received orders to investigate a letter from a soldier claiming that U.S. troops were shooting Vietnamese civilians "indiscriminately" and torturing prisoners.

  Without contacting the letter-writer, Powell submitted a dismissive memo asserting that "relations between Americal soldiers and the Vietnamese people are excellent." Actually, by then the Americal Division had been responsible for some of the most heinous atrocities of the war, including My Lai.

- As a top deputy of then-Secretary of Defense Caspar Weinberger, Powell oversaw the Army's transfer of 4,508 TOW missiles to the CIA in January 1986. About 2,000 of those missiles became part of the arms-for-hostages swap with Iran—a transaction that Powell helped to hide from Congress and the public.

- Soon after becoming President Reagan's national security adviser in 1987, Powell established himself as a point man for U.S. efforts to overthrow the government of Nicaragua.

  Traveling to the region in January 1988, Powell threatened a cutoff of U.S. aid to any Central American nation balking at continued warfare by contra guerrillas in Nicaragua. He pushed for U.S. financing of the contras and worked to sabotage the peace process initiated by Costa Rica's president, Oscar Arias.

- On Dec. 20, 1989—three months after Powell became chairman of the Joint Chiefs of Staff—the United States invaded Panama, killing hundreds of civilians in the first

hours. That day, Powell proclaimed: "We have to put a shingle outside our door saying, 'Superpower lives here.'"

The Organization of American States voted 20-1 to criticize the invasion. But Powell saw it as a great way to guard against Pentagon budget cuts. He "emerged as the crucial figure in the decision to invade" Panama, the British newspaper correspondent Martin Walker reported from Washington. "Among his military peers," the reporter noted, Powell "may yet go down as the man who saved the Pentagon's budget."

- Six months after the bloodletting in Panama boosted the U.S. military's stock at home, Powell delivered a speech charging that if Congress cut the Bush administration's proposed military budget of $303 billion, "you will force us to start breaking the back of our armed forces."

- In 1992, Gen. Powell took the extraordinary step of publishing articles—promoting his own views of foreign policy and appropriate military intervention—in the *New York Times* and the quarterly *Foreign Affairs*.

- Later on in his stint as head of the Joint Chiefs of Staff, Powell moved closer to insubordination. Defying the commander in chief in early 1993, Powell went public with fervent opposition to ending discrimination against gays in the military. Powell spread the word that he'd resign if President Clinton didn't back down on the issue.

During the early 1990s, Powell did a great deal to harm the principle of civilian authority over the military. In theory he served under the command of Presidents Bush and Clinton. In reality, Powell became a military tail that often wagged the civilian dog.

A former chief historian of the U.S. Air Force, Richard H. Kohn, calls Powell "the most powerful military leader since George C. Marshall"—and "the most political since Douglas MacArthur."

Writing in the conservative *National Interest* last year, Kohn concluded: "It was under Colin Powell's tenure that civilian control eroded most since the rise of the military establishment in the 1940s and 1950s."

When we interviewed him a few days ago, Kohn was emphatic: "The trend in the last 25 years has been a weakening of civilian control of the military, and we've seen it most glaringly in the last 10 years."

As the nation's highest-ranking military officer, Colin Powell played a central role in undermining civilian authority over the armed forces. Now, as he considers a run for the White House, journalists have a responsibility to scrutinize his record.

September 6, 1995

Ted Koppel—
Myth vs. Reality

Now that Ted Koppel has completed his publicity blitz for a new book about *Nightline*, the famed ABC anchor is more of a media idol than ever. On one network after another, interviewers kept treating Koppel as journalistic royalty. But this media prince is not what he's cracked up to be.

Koppel is legendary as an intrepid questioner who stalks the truth. And—judging from his recent book tour—Koppel's colleagues in the national media are among his biggest fans. Forget softball questions. Koppel fielded beachballs.

Whether the interviewer was Larry King or Sam Donaldson, the inquiries were fawning and the accolades profuse. Nor did National Public Radio provide a respite from Koppel idolatry: *Fresh Air* host Terry Gross went into rhapsodies about her guest's brilliance. Clearly, she had come not to query Koppel but to praise him.

If Koppel seems like an ideal reporter, that's because we confuse style with substance. He gravitates to power brokers — and for independent journalism, that's a fatal attraction. As *Newsweek* observed a decade ago, Koppel "makes viewers feel that he is challenging the powers-that-be on their behalf"—yet he "is in fact the quintessential establishment journalist."

Long ago, Koppel declared himself "proud to be a friend of Henry Kissinger" and ranked his pal (who orchestrated bloody foreign-policy deceptions from Vietnam to Chile) as "certainly one of the two or three great secretaries of state of our century." Such biases infuse Koppel's TV work, as when he told *Nightline* viewers in April 1992: "If you want a clear foreign-policy vision, someone who will take you beyond the conventional wisdom of the moment, it's hard to do any better than Henry Kissinger."

ABC News ads have referred to Koppel as a "TV statesman." That's fitting. For the anchor of *Nightline*, the line between journalism and U.S. diplomatic efforts is thin indeed.

Asked by *Life* magazine in 1988 if he'd like to be secretary of state, Koppel responded affirmatively and commented on his qualifications: "Part of the job is to sell American foreign policy, not only to Congress but to the American public. I know I could do that." He has already amassed plenty of experience.

During the late 1980s, our associates at the media watch group FAIR conducted a 40-month study of *Nightline*—865 programs in all. The two most frequent guests were (surprise!) Kissinger and another former secretary of state, Alexander Haig. On shows about international affairs, U.S. government policy makers and ex-officials dominated the *Nightline* guest list. American critics of foreign policy were almost invisible.

Koppel didn't see a problem. "We are governed by the president and his cabinet and their people," he fired back. "And they are the ones who are responsible for our foreign policy, and they are the ones I want to talk to." The public needs wide-ranging democratic discourse, not a conveyor belt for elite opinion, but the distinction seems to be lost on Koppel and many other big-name journalists.

Even when Koppel does expose official deception, he's apt to do so years too late—debunking propaganda that he helped spread in the first place. For insight into Koppel's rise up the TV news ladder, consider an incident when he was on a lower rung as ABC's Southeast Asia bureau chief.

From 1969 to 1971, Koppel paid several visits to the southern Laos site of Pakse, where CIA and U.S. military personnel—in an operation kept secret from the American public—were assisting and directing continuous bomb runs by the Laotian air force. "These guys were all in civilian clothes," Koppel told us in a 1990 interview. "None of them admitted to being in the military—or with the CIA, for that matter. They all claimed to be civilian contract employees."

Koppel acknowledged that, at the time, he knew the facts were otherwise: "I may have known that, but I wasn't in a position to prove it." His news reports made no mention of the CIA and U.S. military involvement, even though it was central to the bombing that he witnessed.

Walter J. Smith, a U.S. Air Force officer at Pakse, was present when Koppel showed up with a cameraman at the base officers' club. Smith heard Koppel stress that he would not dislodge the official fig-leaf: "In effect, he was saying, 'I'm not going to tell the truth no matter what happens.'"

A quarter-century later, Walter Smith—now an instructor at Cabrillo College in California—is very willing to talk about what happened. But Smith doesn't expect much interest from mainstream journalists. No need to tarnish the halo of a media icon.

July 3, 1996

The Brave New World
of Bill Gates

This month [December 1996] began with yet another glossy tribute to Microsoft's visionary leader. *Newsweek* devoted seven gaga pages to Bill Gates—"the most powerful single figure in the business world today"—and proclaimed that we're nearing "the Microsoft Century."

Superlatives are routine when media outlets describe the 41-year-old CEO and his software feats. Meanwhile, corporate rivals grouse and moan. But star-struck journalists and envious competitors don't shed much light on the downsides of the Microsoft mind-set.

The brave new world of Bill Gates—transfixed with high-tech form over human content—has little room for social vision. What we get are endless variations of the notion that ever-more-clever digital technology will make life wondrous for paying customers.

These days, Gates says that Microsoft's focus on the Internet will enable the firm to be "intimate" with consumers by maintaining on-line communication: "The relationship, even on productivity software, is a lot more intimate and ongoing."

Incessant techno-babble often drowns out what we used to call critical thinking. As for the next generation, little Johnny or Mary—or Dylan or Chelsea—can't get a hug from their Pentium computer or 28.8 modem or full-color graphics. No hypertext will ever talk with a child as well as a loving relative or friend might. And there's no software on the horizon that can begin to substitute for the soft touch of a parent's hand.

These are not big considerations in the projections for the Microsoft Century. With all the drum-beating about the genius of Bill Gates, this country's media echo chamber is remarkably quiet about values that cannot be put on a spreadsheet.

"The great triumphs of propaganda have been accomplished, not by doing something, but by refraining from doing," Aldous Huxley observed a half-century ago. "Great is truth, but still greater, from a practical point of view, is silence about truth."

Amid all the accolades for trailblazer Gates, we rarely hear about the moral sinkholes of his road ahead. In the quest for market share, less acquisitive concerns get lip service. It's symbolic that Gates—after amassing $20 billion of personal wealth—remains eager to become even richer in a world of rampant poverty.

Last summer, Microsoft and NBC launched a major joint project, MSNBC, combining a new cable TV network and a site on the World Wide Web. Such media ventures may seem to enhance choices, but they actually post more intrusive sentries —"gatekeepers"—along the information superhighway.

When MSNBC premiered, Tom Brokaw spoke of the need to manage cyberspace for young people. "We can't let that generation and a whole segment of the population just slide away out to the Internet and retrieve what information it wants without being in on it," Brokaw told an interviewer.

With uncommon candor, the NBC anchor added: "I also believe strongly that the Internet works best when there are gatekeepers. When there are people making determinations and judgments about what information is relevant and factual and useful. Otherwise, it's like going to the rainforest and just seeing a green maze."

But the biggest players in cyberspace aren't merely guiding us through the media terrain—they're altering it in fundamental ways, bulldozing through certain areas, pointing us in some directions and away from others. In effect, Microsoft is bent on selling us the windows through which we perceive the world.

Consider the comments of Silicon Valley investor Michael Moritz, quoted in the Dec. 2 edition of *Newsweek*: "It's difficult to think of a company in the history of the world that's positioned to influence so many aspects of life as Microsoft is at the end of the 20th century. In terms of a civilized world, you'd have to go back to the Roman Empire to find any organization that had as great a reach as Microsoft has today."

Of course, every media story includes the proverbial "both sides." So, *Newsweek* tells us a bit about the "Anti-Bills" —executives at software outfits like Netscape and Oracle who resent Bill Gates. But they don't really object to the media-monopolizing game; they just want to do better at it themselves.

Missing from standard news accounts are the voices of consumer advocates and media critics with deeper objections. They aren't supposed to have much of a future in the Microsoft Century.

December 4, 1996

Press Critic
Leaves a Legacy of Courage

America's greatest press critic died this month.

He lived to a ripe old age, 104, before his last breath on July 2 [1995]. Yet we're still in mourning for George Seldes.

"The most sacred cow of the press is the press itself," Seldes said. And he knew just how harmful media self-worship could be.

Born in 1890, George Seldes was a young reporter in Europe at the close of World War I. When Armistice Day came, he broke ranks with the obedient press corps and drove behind the lines of retreating German troops. For the rest of his life, he remained haunted by what took place next.

Seldes and three colleagues secured an interview with Paul von Hindenburg, the German field marshal. Seldes asked what had ended the war. "The American infantry in the Argonne won the war," Hindenburg responded, and elaborated before breaking into sobs.

It was an enormous scoop. But allied military censors blocked Hindenburg's admission, which he never repeated in public.

The story could have seriously undermined later Nazi claims that Germany had lost the war due to a "stab in the back" by Jews and leftists. Seldes came to believe that the interview, if published, "would have destroyed the main planks of the platform on which Hitler rose to power." But the reporters involved "did not think it worthwhile to give up our number-one positions in journalism" by disobeying military censors "in order to be free to publish."

Decade after decade, Seldes offended tyrants and demagogues, press moguls and industrialists and politicians. His career began in the mainstream press. During the 1920s, he served as the *Chicago Tribune*'s bureau chief in Berlin, and spent years in Russia and Italy.

Seldes covered many historic figures firsthand, from Lenin and Trotsky to Mussolini. When Seldes wrote about them, he pulled no punches.

As a result, in 1923, Bolshevik leaders banished him from the fledgling Soviet Union. Two years later, he barely made it out of Italy alive; Mussolini sent Black Shirt thugs to murder the diminutive Seldes, small in stature but towering with clarity.

In 1928, after 10 years with the *Tribune*, Seldes quit. The last straw came with the newspaper's selective publication of his dispatches from Mexico: Articles presenting the outlooks of U.S. oil companies ran in full, but reports about the contrary views of the Mexican government did not appear.

Seldes went independent, and became a trailblazing press critic. Starting in 1929, he wrote a torrent of books—including *You Can't Print That*, *Lords of the Press* and *Freedom of the Press*—warning of threats to the free flow of information in the United States and around the world. The press lords, he showed, were slanting and censoring the news to suit those with economic power and political clout.

Like few other journalists in the 1930s, Seldes shined a fierce light on fascism in Europe—and its allies in the United States. Seldes repeatedly attacked press barons such as William Randolph Hearst and groups like the National Association of Manufacturers for assisting Hitler, Mussolini and Spain's Gen. Francisco Franco.

George Seldes and his wife, Helen, covered the war between Franco's fascists and the coalition of loyalists supporting the elected Spanish government. A chain of East Coast daily newspapers carried the pair's front-line news dispatches—until pressure from U.S. supporters of Franco caused the chain to drop their reports.

After reporting from war-torn Spain, with fascism spreading across much of Europe, Seldes returned to the United States. From 1940 to 1950, he edited the nation's first periodical of media criticism—called *In fact*—a weekly which reached a circulation of 176,000 copies.

In fact

AN ANTIDOTE FOR FALSEHOOD
IN THE DAILY PRESS

GEORGE SELDES, Editor
Victor Weingarten, Associate

IF YOUR NAME IS ADDRESSED
IN RED SEE PAGE THREE

NEW DECEPTIONS ARE CHARGED TO READER'S DIGEST; US PUBLIC IS PROPAGANDIZED FOR REACTION

Press Kills Taft-Hartley Expose .... p 3

(No. 379) Vol. XVI, No. 15.
January 12, 1948

Publishers vs Labor

Are YOU Doing Anything To Fight Reaction?

George Seldes, at 102, was still keeping up with media criticism.

Many of his stands, lonely at the time, were prophetic. Beginning in the late *1930s*, for example, Seldes excoriated the American press for covering up the known dangers of smoking while making millions from cigarette ads. He was several decades ahead of his time.

What happened to *In fact*? The *New York Times* obituary about Seldes simply reported that it "ceased publication in 1950, when his warnings about Fascism seemed out of tune with rising public concern about Communism." *In fact*, however, fell victim to an official vendetta.

One FBI tactic was to intimidate readers by having agents in numerous post offices compile the names of *In fact* subscribers. Such tactics were pivotal to the newsletter's demise. Also crucial was the sustained barrage of smears and red-baiting against *In fact* in the country's most powerful newspapers.

Somehow it's appropriate that the *New York Times* would get it wrong in the obituary about *In fact*'s extraordinary editor. For a long time, as Seldes recalled in his autobiography *Witness to a Century*, it was *Times* policy—ordered by managing editor Edwin L. James—"never to mention my newsletter or my books or my name." In 1934, Seldes had testified for the Newspaper Guild in a labor-relations suit against the *Times*, "and James frankly told me on leaving the hearing that he would revenge himself in this way."

In 1988, during a delightful spring afternoon with George Seldes at his modest house in a small Vermont town, we discussed that *Times* embargo on publishing his name. When we quipped, "Hell hath no fury like a paper-of-record scorned," he laughed heartily, his eyes twinkling as they did often during a six-hour discussion.

We asked how he'd found the emotional strength to persevere. Seldes replied, matter-of-factly, that uphill battles come with the territory of trying to do good journalistic work.

This month, the death of George Seldes underscored major-media disinterest in legacies of journalistic courage. *Time* magazine devoted 40 words to his passing; *Newsweek* didn't mention it at all.

As a press critic, George Seldes picked up where Upton Sinclair left off. From the 1930s onward, Seldes was the Diogenes whose light led the way for new generations of journalists eager to search for truth wherever it might lead. The muckraker I.F. Stone aptly called Seldes "the dean and 'granddaddy' of us investigative reporters."

We will always be indebted to George Seldes. The best way to repay him is to live up to the standards he set for himself.

[1996 saw the release of the acclaimed documentary *Tell the Truth and Run: George Seldes and the American Press*, produced and directed by Rick Goldsmith of Berkeley, California.]

July 12, 1995

Investigative Journalism
vs.
Conventional Wisdom

Imagine working as an investigative reporter in the nation's capital and breaking some of the biggest stories of the 1980s.

You win the prestigious George Polk Award for exposing a CIA assassination manual that has been distributed to U.S.-backed contra guerrillas in Nicaragua. The next year, you're a finalist for the Pulitzer Prize and you receive a slew of other awards.

In June 1985, you write the first article about a Marine colonel named Oliver North and reveal that he's running a secret intelligence operation out of the White House. And you continue to produce well-documented articles about clandestine actions later known as the Iran-contra scandal.

But your supervisors at Associated Press get skittish. In late 1985, when you team up with a colleague to write a comprehensive exposé of drug-trafficking by the Nicaraguan contras, AP editors block the story—which only sees the light of day when AP's Spanish-language wire distributes it by mistake. Later, you find out that your boss has been conferring with North on a regular basis.

In 1987, after 10 years with AP in Washington, you quit to become a staff correspondent for *Newsweek*—where you write the first story linking the Oval Office to a cover-up of the Iran-contra affair. You go on to pull the lids off a domestic propaganda apparatus overseen by CIA Director William Casey, the CIA's covert political operations inside Nicaragua, and hidden deals between the U.S. government and Panamanian dictator Manuel Noriega.

Before long, however, *Newsweek*'s editors are slamming on the brakes. They don't seem to want you to dig too deeply or investigate too thoroughly. Soon they're insisting that you abide by Washington's conventional wisdom *even when you've amassed documentation that disproves it.*

Robert Parry doesn't have to imagine any of this. He lived it.

Today, the 46-year-old Parry is pursuing a path that led him out of mainstream media—and into cyberspace. A few weeks ago [in December 1995], he founded what may be America's first on-line magazine of investigative journalism.

Unlike Michael Kinsley, the high-profile pundit who recently took a job with Microsoft to develop an on-line magazine, Parry has no interest in supplying the Internet with new twists on conventional wisdom. Nor does Parry have the backing of a company with deep pockets.

In fact, there's no money behind *The Consortium*, which Parry offers as "an investigative magazine distributed free on the World Wide Web—at http://www.delve.com/consort.html—and by subscription to those who prefer copies by e-mail, fax or mail." (*The Consortium*, Suite 102-231, 2200 Wilson Blvd., Arlington, VA 22201.)

The same attitude that caused Parry to leave AP and *Newsweek* is now guiding his current activities. What distinguishes Parry's project from the mass media's cyber-ventures is his passionate belief that journalism has a responsibility to follow the trail of the truth, wherever it leads.

Parry's 1992 book—*Fooling America: How Washington's Power Brokers Manipulate the Conventional Wisdom to Mislead Journalists, Congress and the American People*—probably ensured that he'll get no job offers from media outfits like *Newsweek*. He deftly skewers the magazine's top editors with firsthand accounts of behind-the-scenes deference to powerful politicians. As far as Washington's media elite is concerned, he'll never eat a power lunch in their town again.

That seems to be OK with Robert Parry. As far as *he's* concerned, journalists shouldn't be socializing with the high-and-mighty anyway.

The lead story in *The Consortium*'s first issue of 1996 recounts how a congressional panel bungled—or covered up—an inquiry into charges that high officials in Ronald Reagan's 1980 presidential campaign interfered with President Carter's efforts to secure the release of 52 American hostages in Iran.

Two years ago, a House task force chaired by Rep. Lee Hamilton (D-Ind.) issued a report saying that it found "no credible evidence" to support the charges of Republican dirty tricks. But now Parry has unearthed documents showing that the task force suppressed incriminating CIA testimony and excluded evidence of big-money links between wealthy Republicans and Carter's Iranian intermediary, Cyrus Hashemi.

Parry's new journalistic breakthrough is mainly based on U.S. government documents. How did he find them? He kept searching—and, early this winter, literally blew the dust off thousands of pages stored in cardboard boxes inside a converted ladies' room near the parking garage of the Rayburn House Office Building on Capitol Hill.

"An intimidating array of individuals and forces wanted President Carter ousted from the White House in 1980," Parry reports. "Some were driven by ambition; others by money; and still others by revenge. Together, they were overpowering. Newly revealed documents, meant to stay hidden from the public, now show the interlocking relationships that operated behind the facade of American democracy."

So far—despite the significance of the documents Parry has brought to light in recent weeks—national news outlets have ignored them. Parry isn't surprised. "Mainstream media cannot deal with the new information because it clashes with the conventional wisdom," he says. What's more, the story "has no active political promoters and requires some mastery of details. So the bogus history of the era is allowed to continue."

It's a shame that big media outlets haven't been more supportive of Robert Parry's talents. But thank goodness he is persevering as a journalist.

January 10, 1996

Jim Hightower:
Radio Populist to be Muzzled?

The most distinctive new voice on talk radio is in danger of being silenced.

Populist Jim Hightower has built a following on 150 stations nationwide during the last 16 months—while breaking most of the rules for talk radio hosts. Instead of shouting, he speaks with a soft Texas twang. He actually lets callers who oppose him be heard. And his barbs are not aimed at women, gays, minorities or the poor—but at the rich and powerful.

Other talk hosts fulminate about "welfare queens." Hightower dwells on the "welfare kings"—the Fortune 500.

Hightower has become talk radio's unabashed advocate for blue-collar workers, pensioners, family farmers and middle-class consumers. The real political spectrum, Hightower contends, is not right-to-left: "It's top-to-bottom, and the vast majority of people aren't even in shouting distance of the economic and political powers at the top."

Although he's been likened to Will Rogers, Hightower *has* met some men he didn't like—those who rip off workaday Americans. Hightower stands up to the powers-that-be on behalf of the powers-that-ought-to-be.

The bad news is that Disney's ABC Radio Networks has decided this month [September 1995] to end its syndication of Hightower's talk show. His removal from talk radio would be enough to wipe the smile off of even Will Rogers' face.

With a progressive populist message that bridges racial gaps (he dismisses California Gov. Pete Wilson, the crusader against affirmative action, as "George Wallace in a Brooks Brothers suit"), Hightower has a rare ability to reach conservatives. During the Reagan era, he was elected twice to Texas statewide office as agriculture commissioner.

Originating from his hometown of Austin, Hightower's talk show offers thorough, well-documented analysis of bread-and-butter issues, such as: NAFTA, the Mexico bailout, the export of U.S. jobs to cheap-labor countries and the corporate safety net that undergirds Newt Gingrich's political career.

The country's first investigative talk show begins with Hightower's own newscast—featuring "Follow the Money" segments on campaign finance, the "Hog Report" on corporate/political greed, and sharp "Eye on Newt" pieces.

Hightower has a novel idea for the 1996 presidential campaign: "Like NASCAR race drivers or PGA golfers, why not require each of the candidates to cover their clothing, briefcases and staff with the logo patches of their corporate sponsors?"

Exposing a recent federal giveaway to a mining company that donated $120,000 to Congress members, Hightower commented: "Under Sen. [Larry] Craig's bill, Cyprus-Amax would pay only $1,000 for a piece of Colorado land that holds $3 billion worth of minerals. They paid 120 times more to buy Congress than they'll pay for the land!... That's why big corporations are so bullish on Congress."

Jim Hightower's show has gotten more raucous since Gingrich—"a guy who can strut sitting down"—ascended to the House speakership. "The higher up the ladder the monkey climbs," Hightower says, "the more you see of its ugly side."

After Bell South, a major financial backer of Gingrich, hired the speaker's daughter, Hightower commented: "Bell South is another corporation that knows that if you want to ring-up The Newt, you don't do it with a telephone—but with a cash register."

During almost every hour of his show, Hightower makes a "Connection"—providing the phone number of a social change organization that's working to address the problem discussed. "Don't just get agitated," exhorts Hightower, "get to agitating." The call-in number to his show is 1-800-AGITATE.

Although he deserves recognition for his wisdom about economic power, Hightower is far better known for his rollicking one-liners:

- "Ronald Reagan's idea of a good farm program was *Hee Haw*," quipped Hightower, who launched environmentally conscious programs in Texas for family farmers.

- "George Bush was born on third base and decided that he'd hit a triple," Hightower declared during his riotous speech at the 1988 Democratic convention.

Hightower also mocks fence-straddling Democrats.

- "There's nothing in the middle of the road but yellow stripes and dead armadillos."

- When Bill Clinton assembled his team of economic advisers, Hightower dubbed it "the Wall Street firm of Bentsen, Rivlen, Altman and Rubin."

Hightower's main target is corporate America, including some of the same companies that are potential sponsors of national talk shows. He once said of price-gouging pharmaceutical firms: "They're making enough profit to air-condition hell."

While he's attracted uncommon sponsors like labor unions and *Mother Jones* magazine, his show has been hobbled by a lack of marketing from the ABC network and undermined by right-wing management at ABC mega-stations in New York and Los Angeles.

"Listeners like the Hightower show," says respected radio consultant Jon Sinton, who helped launch the program. "But it makes big companies nervous."

Now, efforts are underway to get Hightower's talk show picked up by another network or syndicate, perhaps Infinity's Westwood One, CBS or SW/Sony Worldwide. (Meanwhile, his two-minute radio commentaries are still heard daily on 70 stations.)

The Hightower termination contradicts talk radio's claim of being America's "national town hall." Something's wrong with a medium that can find so much room for Rush Limbaugh and dozens of Limbaugh clones and wannabees—but no space for the one-of-a-kind Jim Hightower.

[In September '96, a year after he was terminated by Disney/ABC, Hightower returned to talk radio with a daily show on the United Broadcasting Network, a new venture partly financed by the United Auto Workers union.]

September 20, 1995

Jim Hightower displays cereal box in speech decrying agribusiness greed.

Part X
The Reign
of the "Dixiecan"Congress

The forces of the political right have dug in for a long stay atop Capitol Hill, where they set much of the national agenda in the mid-1990s. Newt Gingrich and his "revolution" have faced obstacles—congressional opposition, the ethics committee, public interest lobbies. But remarkably few impediments have come from independent reporting by mainstream media.

Press Corps
Out to Lunch in First 100 Days

With the first 100 days of the congressional session behind us [in 1995], the press is awash in analysis of Newt Gingrich and the Republican-led Congress, asking: *How did they do?*

The question could be turned around and aimed at journalists: *How well did news media perform in the first 100 days?*

Some journalists did well—stripping away rhetoric to clarify complicated issues. For example, several reporters exposed that congressional attacks on "unfunded mandates" were often end-runs around popular environmental protection laws; that "tort reform" could deny injured workers and consumers access to the courts; and that the capital gains tax cut would benefit only about 8 percent of American families.

Gingrich probably had these independent journalists in mind when he denounced major newspapers for harboring "socialists."

But most reporters seemed content to be aboard Gingrich's speeding train — acting more like stenographers than journalists.

Perhaps the clearest example is the school lunch debate. The House passed a bill that would reduce the amount of food available to school kids. Taking food out of the mouths of children is something that Republicans are understandably defensive about.

So they've taken the offensive...with a big lie, repeated endlessly. And most reporters have ducked and gotten out of their way.

The lie is that—under the GOP's plan—funding will *increase* 4.5 percent next year and succeeding years. In broadcasts and press quotes, Gingrich has claimed "we raised school lunches 4.5 percent for five years." He called the charge that Congress is cutting the program "one of the most horrendously disgusting examples of demagogy I have ever seen."

The 4.5 percent yearly increase for school lunches has been stated as fact by Republican leaders, in news reports quoting those leaders, and in conservative editorials and commentary. Pundits from George Will to John Sununu to Mona Charen have asserted the figure. Charen huffed: "Everyone is entitled to his opinion, but not to his own facts."

Here are the facts.

The legislation that passed the House establishes a school nutrition block grant—combining funds from several federal programs into one grant that will go to the states. The block grant covers not only the school lunch program, but the school breakfast program and portions of programs for summer meals, before-and-after-school snacks, and low-cost milk for schools that don't serve meals.

This year's Congressional Budget Office figures show that these programs currently cost $6.52 billion. The Gingrich block grant allocates $6.68 billion for next year, an increase of only 2.5 percent.

Since inflation is running at roughly 3 percent—and school enrollment is rising—the block grant will cut the amount of food getting to kids through school-based nutrition programs next year.

Under the current food programs (replaced by the block grant bill), funding automatically rises with increases in food costs and school enrollment—and the support level for every kid in need is constant.

If Republican leaders think too much is spent on school-based nutrition programs, they should say so. They shouldn't claim a bogus 4.5 percent yearly increase.

Where did they get that figure? They apparently concocted it, as we learned after obtaining a revealing "worksheet" prepared by the House Economic and Educational Opportunities Committee. For cash outlays to "the school lunch program" to increase by 4.5 percent, other nutritional programs within the block grant would have to be reduced—some by as much as 34 percent.

But there's nothing in the legislation that mandates states cut certain food programs so that they can increase school lunch outlays by 4.5 percent. Indeed, the idea behind block grants —as touted by Republicans —is to let local authorities make their own

decisions. When we asked Committee staffers to explain their statistical sleight of hand, we received no answer.

One of the few journalists to press for an answer was Cox News Service reporter Andrew Mollison, who wrote that a House Republican Conference spokesman admitted the 4.5 percent figure was wrong.

Not only are the Republican figures wrong, says Robert Greenstein of the independent Center on Budget and Policy Priorities, but so are their claims that block grant funds will better target food to those in need. Almost 90 percent of federal school-nutrition funds now benefit low-income children; the block grant requires only that 80 percent benefit such kids.

The law now mandates that children near or below the poverty line receive lunch free. This would not be true under the block grant bill.

No Republican has been more out to lunch about school lunches than the media's loudest commentator, Rush Limbaugh. On March 10, he rallied his followers: "Today, we're going to give you marching orders...to follow us in lock-step." Brandishing the 4.5 percent figure, Limbaugh alleged a media "conspiracy to spread disinformation" about Republicans—"a total brainwashing equaled only by the worst days of Stalin, of Pravda, of Tass."

The truthful one urged his millions of listeners to phone news outlets: "All you say to them is—'Stop lying about the school lunch program, thank you'—and hang up."

Maybe the thousands of such calls received by journalists had nothing to do with the timid and inadequate coverage of the issue. There's another explanation: Reporters simply didn't bother to look up the numbers.

April 12, 1995

Gingrich and the Susan Smith Case: Forgive and Forget?

Newt Gingrich has gotten away with it. Again.

Even after a South Carolina jury declared Susan Smith guilty of murdering her two sons, reporters are not pressing Gingrich about the Smith case. Many seem to have forgotten that nine months ago, he loudly proclaimed the infanticide to be a campaign issue.

Back in November [1994], the motor-mouthed Gingrich had much to say about the case—offering a treatise so wrong-headed that it's almost laughable. Except there's nothing funny about the Susan Smith tragedy—or Gingrich's attempt to exploit it for election-eve advantage.

Here's what Gingrich said three days before last November's election—in response to an Associated Press reporter who asked him how the campaign was going: "Slightly more moving our way. I think that the mother killing the two children in South Carolina vividly reminds every American how sick the society is getting and how much we need to change things."

Gingrich concluded, "The only way you get change is to vote Republican. That's the message for the last three days."

Two days later, less than 24 hours before the polls opened, Gingrich defended his comments on the Smith case as no different than what he'd been saying for years—that violence and related ills arise from a Democratic-controlled political system: "We need very deep change if we're going to turn this country around."

Asked if the change he was offering the country would stop killings like those in South Carolina, he replied, "Yes. In my judgment, there's no question."

Today, reporters should ask Gingrich an obvious question: Does he still impute blame to the Democrats for Susan Smith's deed?

Journalists might also ask Gingrich about Smith's stepfather, Beverly Russell.

Prior to the kids' disappearance, Russell was busily campaigning not for the depraved Democrats, but for Newt Gingrich and his minions. Russell was a Republican leader in South Carolina and local organizer of Pat Robertson's Christian Coalition.

During the nine days that Susan Smith had the country hunting for a nonexistent black carjacker, Russell urged nationwide prayer for the two missing kids: "All we can do is pray. This is a nightmare."

A prominent businessman and stockbroker, Russell married Smith's mom after she divorced Smith's dad (who later committed suicide). From the age of six, Russell raised Susan Smith in an upper-middle-class, church-going home. Gingrich's campaign comments notwithstanding, the home was free of counterculture and welfare-state influences.

But Susan Smith attempted suicide at age 13, and at age 15 told authorities that her stepdad had been sexually molesting her for at least a year. Her mother helped talk her out of pursuing charges against Russell. (At age 18, she attempted suicide again.)

The child-abuse case against the well-connected businessman smells of a cover-up. It's not known exactly how long the molestation went on, because the case file mysteriously vanished. And Susan Smith was not even represented in court by a lawyer or guardian, as required for minors.

The social-service worker who investigated the molestation testified at the murder trial that although Russell admitted the abuse and agreed to seek counseling, she was "concerned" that law enforcement closed the case so quickly.

Whatever counseling Russell underwent had little impact. The murder trial revealed that he was having sex with his stepdaughter as recently as two months before she killed her kids.

While nothing can begin to excuse the ghastly act of drowning children in a lake, it's clear that Susan Smith suffered far more trauma in her youth than any girl should have to endure.

And most of the trauma was inflicted—not by McGovernik Democrats or welfare bureaucrats—but by an abusive stepfather who publicly championed "family values" and "school prayer" as partisan Republican issues.

The truth is that sexual abuse of children in the home is widespread—and crosses all ideological lines. It's also true that the Child Abuse Prevention and Treatment Act was dismembered this year by Gingrich-led "pro-family" forces in the House.

Newt Gingrich should be pressed to discuss these realities. After all, he's the one who originally declared the Smith case in play as a political football. Journalists shouldn't let him simply drop the ball at his convenience.

Here's a question that should be posed: Mr. Gingrich, were you wrong to try to politicize this tragedy, especially when you hadn't a clue what the facts were?

And let's not forget Gingrich's McCarthy-like effort in 1992 to link the Democratic platform to Woody Allen, then in the news for his affair with the 21-year-old daughter of his longtime companion, Mia Farrow.

Would it be fair politics, someone should ask Gingrich, for Democrats to denounce Republicans today as the "Beverly Russell party"?

Currently talking up a storm on his book tour, Newt Gingrich is getting the red carpet treatment on America's biggest talkshows. It would be refreshing to see an interviewer confront the Speaker of the House on his past effort to lay Susan Smith's murdered kids at the feet of the Democratic Party.

July 26, 1995

The South Rises Again...
On Capitol Hill

Like the "purloined letter" openly displayed in the famous tale by Edgar Allan Poe, a very important new reality is right in front of this nation's political journalists. But, for more than a year now, we've barely noticed it.

To a large extent, Southerners are running Congress.

In the House, the three top Republican leaders all hail from the South. When Speaker Newt Gingrich huddles with majority leader Dick Armey and majority whip Tom DeLay, it's a meeting of a Georgian and two Texans.

Over in the Senate, the majority whip is Trent Lott of Mississippi. For good measure, the Senate's president pro tempore is Strom Thurmond of South Carolina.

The 93-year-old Thurmond, who switched to the Republican Party three decades ago, is an elderly link to the last time Southerners reigned supreme on Capitol Hill. He entered the Senate in the mid-1950s, when the chairmen of key committees were reactionary Southern Democrats known as "Dixiecrats."

Like the Dixiecrats of old, the new "Dixiecans" are the farthest-right bloc in Congress, and they're now ruling the congressional roost—especially in the House, where hyper-conservative Southern Republicans control three crucial committees.

The Ways and Means chairman, Bill Archer, comes from Texas. The Appropriations chairman, Robert Livingston, comes from Louisiana. The Commerce chairman, Thomas Bliley Jr., comes from Virginia.

What does this lineup mean for the national government?

Under the current hierarchy, "House Republicans tend to act even more right-wing than they are," says Bill Magavern, director of Public Citizen's Congress Watch. "Because the House is so tightly controlled by their leadership, the only bills that make it onto the floor are those that have the blessing of a small cadre of Republican leaders and committee chairs."

That "cadre" has been largely hand-picked by Gingrich—who chose many like-minded Southern Republicans.

Livingston's grip on the Appropriations gavel "means a lot less funding for agencies that regulate health, safety and the environment," Magavern told us. "And it also has meant attaching legislative language to spending bills that restricts the abilities of agencies to regulate corporate behavior."

While most Republicans are conservative, House members from the South are more so than their GOP colleagues from other regions. "The Southerners tend to be much more uniformly right-wing," Magavern observed, "and more comfortable blatantly following the wishes of their corporate contributors." He added: "The Southern Republicans have made calculations that they're not going to get support from labor or consumers or African-Americans."

The Dixiecans are passionate advocates of shifting power from Washington to the states. A few decades ago, in an era when appeals to racism were routine for Southern politicians, a similar ideology was known as "states' rights"—a code phrase for resistance to federal civil-rights laws.

Such appeals are no longer keynotes, but they often persist as subtexts. Sent to Congress by comfortably wide margins in most cases, Dixiecans don't seem to care what black voters think of them.

In the South more than anywhere else, whites vote for Republicans and blacks vote for Democrats. Except for the few representatives of black-majority districts, Southern seats in Congress are filled by politicians who feel answerable only to whites. And those whites, on the whole, are the most conservative in the nation.

Meanwhile, the enormous Southern clout in Congress remains unexplored by national media. "They have not picked up on the power of the South in American politics," says Ron Nixon, an editor at the Institute for Southern Studies based in Durham, N.C.

The Reign of the "Dixiecan" Congress

For Nixon, an African-American who has lived his adult life in the South, the bypassed story is ominous. He's alarmed at the chorus of congressional Southerners calling for "resistance" to federal encroachment. For anyone who recalls the rhetoric used against civil rights in the '50s and '60s, it sounds familiar.

Certainly, in 1996, much racial bigotry exists outside the South. And many Southern whites are sincere opponents of racism. Yet, Nixon contends, racism is "most blatant" in the South.

While the South is playing a pivotal role in Congress, news outlets keep missing the story—and many Dixiecans will continue to move the levers of power on Capitol Hill.

March 6, 1996

Part XI
Campaign '96:
Status vs. Quo

The election machinery that returned Bill Clinton to the White House and the Republican majority to Congress was greased with oceans of campaign cash, poll-tested rhetoric and media clichés. Lost in the flood were key questions not asked.

Liberal Pundits
Spread Myths about Dole

Media coverage often depicts Bob Dole as suffering from an acute form of political schizophrenia. The story goes that Dole is so anxious to appease far-right Republicans that he loses touch with his own natural decency.

By the time the GOP finishes its San Diego convention in mid-August, party "spin doctors" will be hailing a triumph for Dole's noble inner core. Ironically, quite a few liberal commentators have helped to prepare the ground for such a PR maneuver—which can only be effective to the extent that the public buys the notion of Dole's innate goodness.

Listen to these liberals: *Washington Post* columnist Richard Cohen recently expressed "great respect for what Dole has been and who he is." After Dole bid the Senate adieu, Lars-Erik Nelson of the New York *Daily News* wrote that "the real Bob Dole stood up" to deliver "his most eloquent, honest and touching speech." Later, *Los Angeles Times* veteran Robert Scheer concluded in a column: "Deep down, Dole is a truly reasonable and decent man."

When liberal pundits claim that what they like about Dole is what's most authentic about him, this amounts to weird projection. For instance: During the Nixon presidency, Dole was an unrelenting Senate advocate for the murderous violence being inflicted on Indochina. If the Vietnam War was a moral abomination, how could one of its most avid—and unrepentant—boosters be a truly "decent man"?

Dole went on to serve the gist of the Reagan-Bush agenda for a dozen cruel years. The fact that some of his Republican colleagues were more extreme does not change Dole's complicity with measures that brought deepening poverty to many Americans and ended up undermining much of this country's middle class.

Across the mainstream spectrum, pundits fail to mention Dole's record of fervent support for deadly White House policies in Central America during the 1980s. Nor do we hear about Dole's continued attempts to justify the assorted crimes known as the Iran-Contra scandal.

In a speech to a February 1993 banquet ("Salute to Caspar Weinberger and the Victims of the Walsh 'Witch Hunt'"), Dole lauded key Iran-contra perpetrators and declared: "I'm proud to say that my definition of a patriot is Caspar Weinberger...Clair George...Elliott Abrams." After railing against Iran-contra special prosecutor Lawrence Walsh, the Kansas senator bragged that he'd gone after Walsh's staffers.

"We checked out a lot of the staff," Dole said. "We found out their political leanings, and we checked on their political contributions." The boast should have caused a media uproar. Instead, the Washington press corps yawned.

Consider the media responses to a pair of biographies released last fall by large publishers. *Bob Dole,* by Richard Ben Cramer, is very flattering. *Senator for Sale,* by Stanley Hilton, is highly critical. During the first half of this year, a Nexis database search shows, major media outlets cited biographer Cramer more than 140 times—and cited biographer Hilton a total of 21 times.

Senator for Sale has gotten scant media attention because its portrait of Dole doesn't fit into the established media frame. The author, a lawyer who was a Senate aide to Dole for nine months until May 1980, faults the media for Dole's "totally inaccurate" image.

"Daily contact enabled me to take a hard look at the kind of man Bob Dole is," Hilton writes. "I was repeatedly struck by the banality and superficiality of his character and personality....He had little interest in details. He didn't like to read. His only real concern seemed to be raising money. He had contempt for common voters. And he believed in nothing."

Hilton's book is filled with solid evidence that Dole has catered to big-money interests throughout his political career. *Senator for Sale* is not flawless—at times the book tries too hard to analyze Dole in psychological terms—but it remains an informative document that delves much deeper than what's apt to pass for political reporting on Dole.

"One of the reasons that the media have continued to spout hagiographic myths about Dole is that they don't really know him," Hilton told us a few days ago. "They just see the side of him that he wants them to see."

July 10, 1996

Bob Dole, campaigning in South Carolina

What's Out of the Question for Debates

It's probably just as well that panels of journalists won't be on stage to question Bill Clinton and Bob Dole during the debates. The vast majority of reporters who end up on national television are dedicated conformists. But what if the debaters had to face questions from journalists who bypass the media herd?

We contacted some independent-minded journalists to find out what they'd want to ask at the upcoming debates if they had the chance. Here are their questions:

- Jill Nelson, former staff writer for the *Washington Post*: "In what ways will your administration address the tremendous rage, alienation and violence prevalent among young people in this nation?"

- John Hess, ex-reporter for the *New York Times*: "As you know, federal tax policy has been redistributing wealth from the poor and the middle class to the rich. What would you do about it?"

- Tara Roberts, an editor at *Essence* magazine: "How will you speak for a community, like young black women, that you don't share any commonalties with? Why should they vote for either of you?"

- Jay Bonasia, director of the National Student News Service: "The General Accounting Office reports that college tuition has increased by 234 percent over the past 15 years, while income has risen just 82 percent and inflation 74 percent. Higher education is increasingly funded by students, not our society. Why is this trend occurring, and what will you do to reverse it?"

- Juan Palomo, religion reporter for the *Austin American-Statesman*: "Both of you have made much of your Christian religion as a foundation of your moral values. Given that, could you tell the American people: At the end of the day, when it's just you and your God—no political consultants, no aides, no adoring supporters—how do you explain to that God those actions resulting from your putting political gain over principle, especially when you know that those actions will hurt, in one way or another, those whom Jesus referred to as 'the least of your brothers'?"

- Andrea Lewis, associate editor, Pacific News Service: "What realistic alternatives do you see for jobless people who are losing access to food stamps and welfare benefits?"

- William Wong, columnist at *AsianWeek* magazine: "Immigrants are being blamed for costing the government too much money, when in fact they contribute a great deal to our economy and to our society as a whole. Where do you draw the line on immigration policy?"

- Emil Guillermo, former host of *All Things Considered* on National Public Radio: "Affirmative action has been under attack in this campaign. If existing laws are overturned, what solutions would you come up with to assure equal opportunity for all?"

- Kim Heron, assistant managing editor of the *Detroit Sunday Journal*, a publication of striking Detroit newspaper workers: "Joblessness — and all the corrosion to the soul that goes with it—is not only high in many ghetto neighborhoods, it is at *unprecedented* levels. Why haven't you proposed an approach that even acknowledges the magnitude of the problem?"

- Patrice O'Neill, executive producer of *We Do The Work* on public television: "Both parties have presented 'family values' as a cornerstone of the '96 campaign. While corporations have swelled investor dividends by downsizing and moving jobs overseas, the bottom line for working families is sinking. Millions of Americans work more than one job—which leaves little time for family—and still live near the poverty line. What kind of accountability should U.S.-based corporations have to American workers and their families? What role would you play as president in holding them accountable?"

- Ben Bagdikian, former national-news editor at the *Washington Post*: "Among the developed industrial countries, Americans are the lowest taxed, counting all kinds of personal taxes. That being so, why have both major parties stressed tax-cutting when this country has deteriorating school buildings and lacks universal health care and other benefits those foreign countries enjoy?"

- Morton Mintz, former *Washington Post* reporter: "The Congressional Budget Office says that Congress could cut federal spending sharply by denying the mortgage-interest deduction to the wealthiest Americans. Limiting the deduction to loans of no more than $300,000 would save $34.8 billion in just five years. Should middle-class homeowners, and renters who can't afford to buy a house in the first place, continue to subsidize mortgage-interest deductions for buyers of the most expensive homes?"

A barrage of these probing questions would be a nightmare for Clinton and Dole. But it's not on their worry list. In the narrow world of big-name journalism, such questions are out of bounds.

September 25, 1996

Dole Reveals Much
by Crying "Liberal Media"

Bob Dole deserves credit for doing more than any other American to damage the myth of "the liberal media." Like the boy who yelled "Wolf!" until the warning lost all credibility, Dole has undermined a key rallying cry of this nation's conservative flock.

In late October [1996], with his campaign nearly unglued, Dole opted to castigate the press for "liberal bias." Perhaps, like the fabled boy tending sheep, Dole craved some favorable attention. But his frantic, repeated outcry was clearly a desperate noise rather than any kind of plausible claim.

It was all too transparent: After turning out to be an abysmal candidate, Dole had no one to blame but himself—or the news media.

Dole was seeking applause from believers in the "liberal media" mythology. Many media venues—from talk-radio programs to TV chat shows to opinion pages—routinely feature commentators who denounce the media for being insufficiently conservative. But, if the media were really so liberal, why would those denunciations get so much air time and print space?

Facts haven't seemed to matter much. For instance: In news coverage, the most widely quoted and cited think tank in the country is the fervently conservative Heritage Foundation. Nationwide, talk radio is dominated by hosts who go through a daily ritual of blaming America's ills on liberals. The big TV networks are owned by huge firms such as General Electric (NBC), Westinghouse (CBS), Disney (ABC) and Time Warner (CNN), hardly bastions of liberalism.

Actually, what some people mean by "liberal media" is the profusion of TV offerings along the lines of Jerry Springer and Jenny Jones. But such shows are not liberal, they're libertine (and disgusting). Ironically, those salacious and degrading programs exist solely to maximize profits—the central goal of the "free enterprise" system that Dole and fellow conservatives love to extol.

What Bob Dole fails to explain is how the corporate setup he reveres could keep going so wrong. After all, Dole and most other politicians strive to serve the economic interests of the corporations that own the largest media outlets. Top execs at the major networks are as eager for an unbridled "free market" as Dole is.

By attributing his difficulties to "the liberal media," Dole has unwittingly helped to expose the myth's scapegoating function. When right-wing forces run into problems with the public, the reflex is often to blame the media.

Meanwhile, we're told about surveys showing that most reporters vote for Democrats. But what matters is the content of news reporting, not the personal views of journalists. And Republican charges of on-the-job bias are usually baseless.

In the waning days of his campaign, Dole complained that the *New York Times* gave short shrift to evidence of improper contributions from Indonesian tycoons to the Democratic Party. By the time Dole launched his anti-*Times* diatribes, however, the newspaper had published 11 news stories about that scandal — including three articles on the front page. What's more, the *Times* had already printed a pair of editorials criticizing the Indonesian donations, along with several very tough columns by William Safire on the issue.

Rest assured that Dole won't have a single cross word for another Manhattan-based daily. The *New York Post* is a possession of media mogul Rupert Murdoch, who owns many newspapers and magazines as well as book publishing houses, TV stations and the Fox network. Murdoch—who may be the most powerful individual in the media world—has donated $1 million to the California Republican Party this year.

Certainly, the "liberal media" epithet will endure as a moldy canard. But from now on, the phrase is likely to give off a distinct aroma of very sour grapes.

So, we should thank Bob Dole for doing this country a good turn. In the future, millions more Americans will roll their eyes and tune out the next time a politician starts to rant against "the liberal media."

October 30, 1996

Clinton Triumph:
A Big Win for "Ultra-Centrists"

Now that Bill Clinton has sailed to victory, the press is awash in talk about his second term. Many pundits are advising the president to stay with the prevailing winds so that he can continue to triumph as a moderate.

That would please a lot of Americans—including most journalists—who are wary of "ultra-liberals" and "ultra-conservatives." But we lack an appropriate label for the new breed of Democrats bent on hugging the political center as soon as their pollsters can find it.

Let's call them "ultra-centrists."

Moderate on the surface, the ultra-centrists are actually quite extreme about seeking the center of power's gravity. Their dedication to compromise is impressive...to the point of shamefulness. Few principles are so inviolate that they can't be spliced, diced or gutted.

Of course, expediency is an old story in politics. But the Clintonites have a phenomenal knack for shredding their supposed ideals and turning the result into confetti to celebrate their exemplary moderation.

Like much of the Washington press corps, the ultra-centrists see winning as proof of wisdom. More than ever, they are preoccupied with pragmatic matters, such as the lowest common denominator in the political math problem known as the electoral college.

Meanwhile, many in the media business claim to be little more than flies on the national wall. "We're just paid observers," the *Chicago Tribune*'s editorial-page editor told *Newsweek*. But, in tandem with top Democrats and Republicans, news media set the mainstream boundaries—defining what merits repeated attention.

In recent weeks, media piety about campaign contributions has been wondrous to behold. Megabucks have always flowed to politicians—as well as mass media. If it's awful that the Democratic and Republican parties take huge corporate contributions, why is it fine for Tom Brokaw, Peter Jennings and Dan Rather to get millions in pay every year from network owners General Electric, Disney and Westinghouse?

Like their conservative compatriots, ultra-centrists don't ask such questions. Clinton and Al Gore join with GOP leaders to keep dipping into the same well as the big names of TV news. Shared assumptions are compatible with corporate agendas: maximizing profits while minimizing concern for people at the lower rungs of the economic ladder.

In the words of a Nov. 4 [1996] *Washington Post* headline, "Democrats See Future in 'Militant Centrism.'" So, what is "militant centrism"? The *Post* described it as "the drive to force an internal realignment of the national Democratic Party by wresting power from the party's liberal wing."

The Sunday before the election, Clinton spoke at a black church in Tampa while Gore made the rounds of four black churches in Detroit—attending to a core constituency that they'd spent much of the last four years ignoring. Nearly half of African-American children remain below the poverty line; the new welfare "reform" law will make the situation worse.

This year, the media cacophony has all but drowned out voices asking why poverty is so widespread in our country. The same administration that agreed to annual military spending of $266 billion—even more than the Pentagon requested—has made no effort to develop federal programs that could uplift tens of millions of low-income Americans.

Instead, the news media are rife with political clichés, the frequent enemies of meaning. Typically, on election night, Cokie Roberts informed ABC's viewers: "The economy is great." Glib generalizations obscure the people who suffer the truth of evasion's consequences.

Near the end of his victory speech Tuesday night, Clinton declared: "We proclaim that the vital American center is alive and well." On Wednesday, the White House chief of staff, Leon

Panetta, summed up the message from the election returns: "If you want to move forward, move to the vital center."

But, routinely, the center is more craven than vital. In the 1950s and 1960s, the center equivocated during the great battles for civil rights. While the Vietnam War took its tragic toll in blood, the antiwar movement grew because the center could not hold. Since then, with issues ranging from the environment to social justice to human rights, the leaden center has been an albatross weighing heavily against progress.

Days before the election, Clinton used the motto that another incumbent, Ronald Reagan, made famous: "It's morning in America."

Uh-uh. For many of the people shut out of the media fixations, it's mourning in America. The ultra-centrists are fabricating a bridge to the 21st century.

November 6, 1996

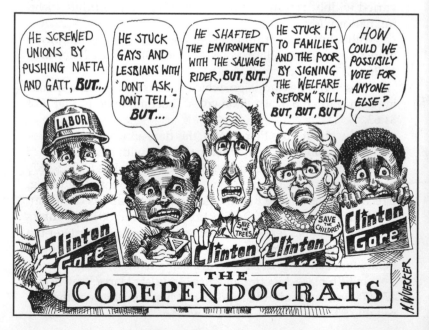

News That Went Unreported: "Dollars Per Vote"

By now, many news reports have analyzed the election results in great detail. On television and in print, we've seen lots of charts and graphs showing the breakdown of votes by gender, race, age, income and a whole lot more. But an important aspect of the election has escaped press attention: the cost of each vote.

"Dollars Per Vote" could be a useful category for putting various campaigns into clearer focus. The public ought to know how much the candidates spent for every vote they received.

After the election, we searched for media coverage of Dollars Per Vote. And searched. And searched. No luck.

So, we did the math ourselves. Here's what we discovered:

In the general election campaign, the Dollars Per Vote varied widely among the seven presidential candidates who ran nationwide.

Bill Clinton's campaign spent $61.8 million of taxpayer money to win 45.6 million votes. So, the "DPV" for Clinton was $1.36.

The Bob Dole campaign, which adhered to the same spending limit, garnered 37.9 million votes. That amounted to a DPV of $1.63.

How about Ross Perot? Well, this time around, the pseudo-populist billionaire accepted federal funds with a ceiling of $29 million and captured just under 8 million votes. His DPV: $3.67.

The man who finished fourth in the presidential balloting, Green Party candidate Ralph Nader, opted to cap his campaign expenditures at $5,000. On Election Day, about 581,000 voters chose him. For Nader—alone among the seven candidates—the spending per vote can't be expressed in dollars. He spent about a penny for each vote. In DPV terms, that's $0.01.

In fifth place, Libertarian Party candidate Harry Browne got 471,000 votes. Available reports put his campaign outlays at roughly $3 million. If so, his DPV was $6.37.

The campaigns for the candidates who brought up the rear—the Taxpayers Party's Howard Phillips and the Natural Law Party's John Hagelin—each reportedly spent in the neighborhood of $2 million. For Phillips, who denounces the Republican Party as too liberal, his 179,000 votes cost $11.17 a piece. For Hagelin, who netted 110,000 votes, the DPV was $18.18.

These DPV figures are ballpark measurements that understate the resources behind the major-party candidates, including "soft money." Well-heeled "issue advocacy" groups and unaffiliated boosters were able to skirt the spending limits. In effect, the Clinton and Dole forces expended several dollars for each vote. Meanwhile, the financial gaps were only part of the imbalance. Let's not forget that Clinton and his GOP rival—as well as, to some extent, Ross Perot—enjoyed enormous advantages in the form of profuse media coverage.

No matter how you slice it, the contrast with Ralph Nader is striking. Even if you include all the money that independent committees paid to promote Nader's candidacy—no more than $200,000—the spending per vote on his behalf totaled, at most, one-third of a dollar.

The evident lack of media curiosity about Dollars Per Vote also extends to thousands of other political races—and state ballot initiatives.

The *New York Times* published a prominent post-election story under a sweeping headline: "From California to Maine, Voters Agreed With the Corporate View on Issues." The news article declared that the latest voting on ballot measures "suggests that Americans' on-again, off-again flirtation with anti-business causes is off again."

The article barely mentioned that victorious industries— ranging from high-tech firms to timber companies to health-care conglomerates—had poured huge amounts of money into winning at the ballot box. Instead, the *Times* emphasized the outlooks of analysts like Brookings Institution savant Thomas Mann. "The public is less angry and less willing to identify with populism," he proclaimed, adding that "there's a certain sobriety out there—a new understanding that we need a strong private sector."

Most voters may be sober, but the businesses ponying up millions to get their way at the polls are quite inebriated with their high-rolling power. In state after state, big-money ad campaigns beat back under-funded efforts to protect consumers, medical patients and the environment. A media spotlight on Dollars Per Vote would illuminate the corruption of the initiative process.

As long as news outlets don't provide us with such information, we're going to have to figure it out for ourselves.

November 13, 1996

Today's Rhetoric
Echoes Past Blather

Some media commentators have contrasted this year's dreary campaign rhetoric with the olden days, when presidential contenders spoke more like true visionaries. But memory lane should not take us on a detour that avoids the shabby side of political icons.

Pundits have chided Bob Dole for lacking the qualities that endeared Ronald Reagan to millions of Americans during the 1980s. Such nostalgia has caused Republican officials in Illinois to start holding annual "Lincoln-Reagan Day" dinners. At this rate, California motorists will find the motto "Land of Reagan" on their license plates—made by prison labor, of course, with each plate bearing the logo of a chain instead of a union bug.

It's telling that so many journalists seem to yearn for the Reaganesque. If Abe Lincoln was the Great Emancipator, the grim truth is that Ron Reagan was the Great Prevaricator. He was also a font of sugared homilies.

The formula has long been bipartisan. Forty years ago, Lyndon Johnson gave fair warning: "You senators and reporters —you better saddle your horses and put on your spurs if you're going to keep up with Johnson on the flag, mother and corruption."

Inevitably, each spoonful of saccharine helps the vile medicine go down. Campaigning in August 1964 as an incumbent president, LBJ reassured the electorate: "Our one desire—our one determination—is that the people of Southeast Asia be left in peace to work out their own destinies in their own way."

In modern American politics, the gold-tongue standard was set by John F. Kennedy. News media still encourage us to revere his soaring cadences. Rarely does anyone have the ill grace to mention that JFK littered his path to the White House with easy bromides and falsehoods.

"I realize that it will always be a cardinal tenet of American foreign policy not to intervene in the internal affairs of other nations—and that this is particularly true in Latin America," Kennedy asserted. The claim was politically astute but historically absurd.

Before he won the presidency in 1960, Kennedy charged that the Soviet Union led the arms race: "Most important of all—and most tragically ironic—our nation could have afforded, and can afford now, the steps necessary to close the missile gap." And Kennedy warned that the Soviets "may well be pulling ahead of us in numbers of long-range jet bombers with a nuclear bomb capacity."

The "missile gap" and the "bomber gap" were calculated fantasies. In fact, the U.S. military had a huge advantage in each category.

Does it matter that Kennedy often wove distortions into the stunning brocade of his oratory? Well, it doesn't matter much in mainstream media. Several decades later, JFK's outsized reputation for eloquence continues to stand in our light. What he said seems to matter much less than how he said it.

Likewise, news media are apt to recall Dwight Eisenhower as a president who spoke in moderate tones. Yet, he was quite willing to go along with demagoguery when it suited his purposes.

Eisenhower pandered to the witch hunters of the McCarthy Era. "To work for the U.S. government is a privilege, not a right," he declared a few weeks before the 1952 election. "And it is the prerogative of the government to set the strictest test upon the loyalty and the patriotism of those entrusted with our nation's safety."

Although Sen. Joseph McCarthy gets the blame for the era that bears his name, it might be more accurately called the Truman Era. With the rationale of pre-empting the rabid Republican right (does this sound familiar?), the incumbent Democratic president signed into law various "loyalty" programs in 1947. Harry Truman put his signature—and his rhetoric—behind measures to shred civil liberties.

Since then, politicians eyeing the White House have rarely failed to invoke the "Give 'em Hell" Truman spirit. They're eager to do so because of his enduring media image as a feisty leader with integrity.

Clinton and Dole deserve condemnation for their fast-talking evasions during the '96 campaign. The sins of predecessors do not excuse their own. But we should not succumb to nostalgia for a wondrous past that never existed.

October 23, 1996

Part XII
Mediated History

Most of what Americans perceive about history—ancient and recent—has been viewed through media lenses. Often the picture seems crisp and reassuring. But, from 1492 to the modern era, the dominant images of past glories owe their endurance to the absence of clear light.

Goodbye, Columbus Day:
Time to End the Myth

At the end of this month, many of us will slip on costumes and fantasy identities for Halloween. When Christmas nears, we'll perpetrate a fiction on our kids about Santa Claus.

But Columbus Day has already arrived—a good time to confront the mythology about the heroic explorer who "discovered" America.

Journalism should help us strip away myths to reveal facts and truths. Yet when it comes to Christopher Columbus, many mainstream pundits—from *New York Times* book reviewers to *Wall Street Journal* editorial writers—hold on dearly to myth. Meanwhile, historians who deal in documentation are denigrated as "politically correct" revisionists.

Columbus had convinced Spain's king and queen to finance his 1492 westward journey to Asia on the grounds that great riches, especially gold, would be found there. The navigator never made it to Asia—ending up instead in the Americas: the Bahamas, then Cuba and Haiti.

The first sailor on the expedition who sighted land was to get a big reward. On October 12, seaman Rodrigo cried out that he'd spotted land—a Bahama island. But Columbus, claiming he'd seen land the evening before, seized the reward himself.

In the revealing log that Columbus kept during his voyage, he described how the friendly Arawak Indians first greeted his ships: "They do not bear arms, and do not know them, for I showed them a sword, they took it by the edge and cut themselves out of ignorance... They would make fine servants... With 50 men we could subjugate them all and make them do whatever we want."

Columbus embarked on a frenzied hunt for imaginary gold fields, using Indian captives: "As soon as I arrived in the Indies, on the first island which I found, I took some natives by force in order that they might learn and might give me information of whatever there is in these parts."

In exchange for bringing back riches to Spain's monarchs, Columbus had been promised 10 percent of all profits and governorship of the land he took control of.

After establishing a fort on Haiti called "Navidad" (Christmas), Columbus returned to Spain—with many Indian prisoners dying aboard ship—to give a glowing report to the royalty in Madrid about what he'd found in the New World.

Columbus described the Indians as "so naive and so free with their possessions" that "when you ask for something they have, they never say no." His report ended with a plea for more support from the Spanish king and queen so he could return from his next voyage to the Indies with "as much gold as they need...and as many slaves as they ask."

Columbus' second expedition was granted 17 ships and 1,200 men in pursuit of gold (which was sparse) and potential slaves (who were plentiful). The result was a holocaust against the native population—as the Spaniards pillaged the Caribbean, island by island.

In 1495, Indians were shipped to Spain as slaves, many dying en route. "Let us in the name of the Holy Trinity," Columbus later wrote, "go on sending all the slaves that can be sold."

But far more Indians were enslaved in their homelands to harvest gold from bits of dust found in streams. Columbus' men ordered everyone over age 13 in a province of Haiti to bring in a quota of gold; Indians who failed had their hands cut off and were left to bleed to death.

The war against the native population was so vicious — including hangings, burnings and then mass suicides—that historians estimate half of the Indians on Haiti (as many as 125,000 people) were dead within a few years. Virtually all were dead within two generations.

Today, media voices that boom the loudest in defense of Columbus—"I don't give a hoot if he gave some Indians a disease that they didn't have immunity against," crowed Rush

Limbaugh—are often the most ignorant. Limbaugh, for example, once asserted that "Columbus saved the Indians from themselves."

History tells a different story. The most important document of the era is the multivolume *History of the Indies* by Bartolome de las Casas—a Spanish priest involved in the conquest of Cuba who owned a plantation employing Indian slaves. But Las Casas had a change of heart and began recording what he'd witnessed.

He described a cooperative Indian society in a bountiful land, a generally peaceful culture that occasionally went to war with other tribes. Yet there'd been no subjugation of the kind brought by Columbus. Writing in the early 1500s, Las Casas detailed how a whole people was basically worked to death— "depopulated"—in utter brutality: men in gold mines, women in the fields.

Las Casas witnessed Spaniards—driven by "insatiable greed"—"killing, terrorizing, afflicting, and torturing the native peoples" with "the strangest and most varied new methods of cruelty." The systematic violence was aimed at preventing "Indians from daring to think of themselves as human beings."

The Spaniards "thought nothing of knifing Indians by tens and twenties and of cutting slices off them to test the sharpness of their blades," wrote Las Casas. "My eyes have seen these acts so foreign to human nature, and now I tremble as I write."

This bloody history might make modern readers tremble— if they had access to it instead of just today's mythology.

It's true that Columbus was a gifted navigator, personally brave and tenacious. But his enterprise—as historian Howard Zinn documents in *A People's History of the United States*—was infused with racism and greed.

Holiday fantasies about jolly old Saint Nick may be harmless. But urging Americans to blithely celebrate Columbus every year is a denial of our past—and an affront to our multicultural present.

October 4, 1995

Media Stampede Led Smithsonian to Set History Aside

"Who controls the past controls the future; who controls the present controls the past."

In sync with that chilling precept from George Orwell's novel *1984*, the battle over an exhibit at the Smithsonian Institution has ended. History lost.

From the outset, news media provided heavy-gauge artillery for the rout. By last summer [1994], a full-scale brouhaha had erupted over the Smithsonian's plans for a 50th anniversary display of the *Enola Gay*, the plane that dropped an atomic bomb on Hiroshima. In short order, realities of the past were in the media cross-hairs.

The Aug. 28 *This Week* telecast on ABC was typical, with George Will leading the charge. "The Smithsonian has some people obviously working for it who shouldn't be," he declared. "They're tendentious and they rather dislike this country and—"

"And ignorant," interjected host David Brinkley.

"And ignorant," Will agreed. He went on: "It's just ghastly when an institution such as the Smithsonian casts doubt on the great leadership we were blessed with in the Second World War."

None of the journalists on the program disagreed. "In the context of the time...the bombing made a great deal of sense," correspondent Cokie Roberts said; raising critical questions about it now "makes no sense at all." And so went most of the media discourse.

Charles Krauthammer denounced exhibit plans in an Aug. 19 *Washington Post* column that excoriated "the forces of political correctness and historical revisionism." The display, he warned, "promises to be an embarrassing amalgam of revisionist hand-wringing and guilt."

Like many other pundits, Krauthammer suggested setting up an *Enola Gay* exhibit like the one accorded the first airplane to cross the Atlantic: "Display it like Lindbergh's plane, with silent reverence and a few lines explaining what it did and when. Or forget the whole enterprise and let the Japanese commemorate the catastrophe they brought on themselves."

But the Japanese people who lived in Hiroshima and Nagasaki did not bring nuclear holocaust on themselves. Perhaps the biggest U.S. media evasion is the avoidance of a basic truth: *Civilians lived in those cities. Hundreds of thousands of them died as a result of the atomic bombings.*

President Truman tried to hide the truth when he announced the Aug. 6, 1945, attack: "The world will note that the first atomic bomb was dropped on Hiroshima, a military base. That was because we wished in this first attack to avoid, in so far as possible, the killing of civilians."

Ironically, only weeks ago the U.S. media supplied profuse and empathetic news accounts of the human suffering after an earthquake took several thousand lives in Kobe. But the same news outlets have done little to acknowledge the humanity of the multitudes of people who died in two other Japanese cities— due not to an act of God, but acts of war.

The nuclear attacks—on Hiroshima and on Nagasaki three days later—signified the completion of a colossal shift in public attitudes. In 1939, when World War II began, wholesale bombing of civilians seemed unconscionable. By 1945 it was widely accepted.

A 1983 statement by U.S. Catholic Bishops urged a "climate of opinion which will make it possible for our country to express profound sorrow over the atomic bombing in 1945. Without that sorrow, there is no possibility of finding a way to repudiate future use of nuclear weapons."

But, evidently, dominant media voices cannot abide any such sorrow.

More than a decade ago, Manhattan Project nuclear physicist Ralph Lapp asked: "If the memory of things is to deter, where is that memory? Hiroshima...has been taken out of the American conscience, eviscerated, extirpated."

Despite the Smithsonian's major changes of exhibit plans in response to the furor from veterans' groups and members of Congress, the media jihad never flagged.

On Nov. 23, the *MacNeil/Lehrer NewsHour* aired a long report heavily dominated by denunciations of the exhibit—and re-aired much of it on Jan. 30 [1995].

George Will—dubbed by the *Wall Street Journal* "perhaps the most powerful journalist in America"—kept banging away in print and on the airwaves. He returned to the subject Jan. 22 [1995] during an interview with the White House chief of staff, Leon Panetta, on ABC's *This Week*. Will accused the Smithsonian of being "evidently incapable of displaying the *Enola Gay*...without turning it into an anti-American exhibit."

The barrage against unpalatable history was not unanimous, but it was pervasive and dominant. As historian Kai Bird noted last fall in the *New York Times*, "A hostile press portrayed the [Smithsonian] curators as anti-American, leftist and motivated by their anti-Vietnam War generational instincts rather than scholarship and archival evidence."

But, as Bird put it, "there is compelling evidence that diplomatic overtures, coupled with assurances on the postwar status of the emperor and the impending entry of the Soviet Union into the war, probably would have led the Japanese to surrender long before an American invasion could be mounted. Unfortunately, all this evidence dribbled out long after orthodoxy had taken root."

Contrary to widespread media assertions, a Japanese surrender did not require the atomic bombings *or* a U.S. invasion of Japan. This is the view of many scholars, including Gar Alperovitz, Martin Sherwin and James Hershberg.

Our nation's mass media rarely allude to ignoble factors in President Truman's decision to order the atomic bombings: a desire to justify the Manhattan Project's enormous wartime expenditure of $2 billion; a goal of rattling nuclear sabers at the Soviet Union; and a wish to measure the impacts of an A-bomb on large urban areas—in other words, nuclear experimentation on human beings.

A physicist who worked on the Manhattan Project, David H. Frisch, later remembered that U.S. military strategists were eager "to use the bomb first where its effects would be not only politically effective but technically measurable."

Manhattan Project director Leslie R. Groves recalled that it was "desirable that the first target be of such size that the damage would be confined within it, so that we could more definitely determine the power of the bomb." For the same reason, criteria for the targeted Japanese cities included absence of previous bombardment.

Fifty years later, this nation apparently still can't face itself in the light of the horrific flashes that turned two Japanese cities into sites of holocausts. Instead of holding up a mirror for us, the mass media keep helping us to look away. That should tell us something about the morality of the atomic bombings of Hiroshima and Nagasaki.

February 22, 1995

Blinded by the Light:
50 Years of Nuclear Boosterism

Fifty years ago, the world's first atomic explosion shattered the desert dawn in New Mexico, just an hour's drive from a town called Truth or Consequences. The date was July 16, 1945.

The world has never been the same.

At first, an official smoke screen surrounded that nuclear detonation; code-named "Trinity," it was part of the supersecret Manhattan Project.

The government's cover story moved on the wires of Associated Press: "An ammunition magazine, containing high-explosives and pyrotechnics, exploded early today in a remote area of the Alamogordo air base reservation, producing a brilliant flash and blast which were reported to have been observed as far away as Gallup, 235 miles northwest."

But three weeks later, when a U.S. plane dropped an atomic bomb on Hiroshima, humanity learned that it had gained the ability to destroy itself.

The unfathomable power of a single warhead shook a routine assumption: that despite the mortality of each individual, the human race would endure. The image of a mushroom cloud evoked unprecedented horror. Yet, nuclear weapons quickly became part of America's political, cultural and economic landscape.

By July 1946—when the U.S. began peacetime testing of A-bombs in the Pacific—the media spin had settled into nuclear boosterism. *Newsweek* provided advance coverage under headlines like "Atomic Bomb: Greatest Show on Earth" and "Significance: The Good That May Come From the Tests at Bikini."

Forty-two thousand U.S. military personnel were within a few miles of the first two explosions at the Bikini atolls. The American press downplayed the Bomb's impact. "Awful as it was," *Time* magazine reported, "it was less than the expectations of many onlookers."

Newsweek remarked: "Man....could sigh with relief. Alive he was; given time and the sanity of nations, he might yet harness for peace the greatest force that living creatures had ever released on this earth."

During the next 16 years, more than 200 mushroom clouds rose over test sites in the Pacific Ocean and the Nevada desert. The fallout ravaged the health of downwind residents from the Marshall Islands to Utah, Nevada and northern Arizona.

Opponents of nuclear tests didn't get much ink or air time in the 1950s—while baby boomers grew up with radioactive isotopes in their bodies, courtesy of American and Soviet nuclear tests spewing fallout to the global winds.

The 1963 Limited Test Ban treaty pushed tests underground. It was a major victory for public health. But bomb testing—and the nuclear arms race—continued, out of sight and out of public mind.

Beginning in the late 1970s, some of the 300,000 U.S. veterans who'd been exposed to above-ground nuclear tests at close range—"atomic veterans"—stepped forward to talk about unusually high rates of cancer, as well as birth defects among their children. Similar evidence has come from nuclear-industry workers, and people living downwind and down river of nuclear facilities.

In 1988, a major scandal rocked the Department of Energy, the federal agency in charge of atomic-weapons plants emitting extensive radioactive pollution. But rather than widening debate over nuclear-arms policy options, the media focus was narrow: How could the country clean up and modernize its weapons assembly line?

In October 1988, *Time* reported that DOE "finally seems bent on reform" and "has taken commendable steps to infuse a safety-conscious attitude at the weapons facilities."

In mid-1989, the newsweekly led off a follow-up article with soothing words: "For 40 years the nation's nuclear weaponry has provided enough security to allow Americans to sleep better at night."

A spate of recent revelations—about government-run radiation experiments on human beings in previous decades—have won widespread media praise for the latest DOE secretary, Hazel O'Leary. At the same time, the Clinton administration continues to pour vast resources into nuclear weaponry.

With bipartisan support, the White House is implementing new multibillion-dollar programs to "upgrade" the nation's nuclear weapons labs. And the administration is pressuring many localities to accept a variety of nuclear wastes—which continue to mount due to ongoing operation of nuclear power and weapons plants.

Meanwhile, although news media hardly seem to notice, some voices keep insisting that it's wrong to build nuclear weapons. One of those voices belongs to Samuel H. Day Jr.

After a journalistic career including jobs as an AP reporter, editor of the *Bulletin of the Atomic Scientists* and managing editor of *The Progressive* magazine, Sam Day found that he could no longer just write news and commentary.

Today, at age 68, Day is in prison. He's serving a six-month sentence for stepping onto the grounds of the U.S. Strategic Nuclear Command headquarters in Nebraska to protest nuclear weapons.

A federal court in Omaha declared Sam Day to be a criminal. But Day pointed out that grave criminality could be seen in the highest offices of the land: "Under international law it is a crime to point weapons of mass destruction at defenseless cities. Under international law, it is the duty of every citizen to do everything possible to prevent such crimes."

The nation's military command, he added, "controls the targeting and launching of many thousands of nuclear warheads, some more than 100 times more powerful than the bomb that destroyed Hiroshima.... And I chose to come here now because, contrary to public opinion and despite the end of the Cold War, our government has not relinquished one iota of its capacity for waging nuclear war. And it has no intention of doing so."

The national news media decided that the arrest, trial and incarceration of Samuel H. Day Jr. did not merit a mention. But,

Sam Day, anti-nuclear crusader, convict, and media non-person

no doubt, many Americans would find meaning in his words, if only they had a chance to hear them:

"I beg for mercy—not for myself, but for the many millions who may some day perish under the mushroom clouds of nuclear weapons launched, in effect, from this very district. I pray for mercy for the children, the old and the sick, the disadvantaged and the disabled who suffer daily, even in the absence of nuclear war, because [they lack] public funds that should be spent for them, rather than siphoned into the coffers of corporations and military services that profit from preparations for nuclear war. And I beg for mercy for the earth, suffocating and dying bit by bit under its mounting burden of permanent, deadly, radioactive poison."

July 5, 1995

Former Defense Secretary McNamara and the Missing Man

When media commentators get tired of passing judgment on Robert McNamara, some might get around to remembering a man who stood next to him, looking out a window of the defense secretary's office—as thousands of antiwar protesters below lay nonviolent siege to the Pentagon on Oct. 21, 1967.

By then, McNamara now says, he had decided that the war was unwinnable. Yet he remained silent as millions of people died in Vietnam and neighboring countries.

But what about the man who stood next to McNamara that Saturday afternoon long ago? We've searched through hundreds of mainstream media articles about the current uproar over McNamara's new book. Only a few even mention Daniel Ellsberg.

Yet it would be logical—and illuminating—to compare the two men.

A quarter-century ago, Ellsberg did what McNamara was never willing to do: denounce the war *during* its murderous frenzy.

In June 1967, McNamara ordered a detailed internal review of U.S. policy-making on Vietnam—but he insisted on secrecy for the results (which documented a pattern of government deception). Ellsberg, who'd been a Defense Department policy analyst and speechwriter for McNamara, leaked the "Pentagon Papers" to the press in 1971.

McNamara subjugated conscience. Ellsberg took heed.

McNamara risked nothing. Ellsberg risked many years — perhaps the rest of his life—in prison on federal espionage charges.

McNamara went on to a prestigious new career as president of the World Bank. Ellsberg moved on to a path of civil disobedience and other forms of nonviolent resistance against the military establishment he had served.

While McNamara was finishing his memoirs in the early 1990s, Ellsberg was launching "Manhattan Project II"—an effort to bring about worldwide nuclear disarmament, putting him at odds with U.S. policy.

And this month [April 1995], while McNamara shuttled from one TV-network studio to another, Ellsberg was busy organizing a "Fast for Commitment to Abolish Nuclear Weapons"—now underway as the United Nations holds a 26-day non-proliferation conference. (Fasters are urging a "global effort to delegitimize and to ban, under international inspection, the possession of nuclear weapons by anyone.")

When Robert McNamara discusses the lessons of Vietnam, he seems pathetic—and still rather clueless. He asserts that his mistakes were "not of values and intentions but of judgment and capabilities." Like many present-day pundits, McNamara bemoans that Washington persisted in an "unwinnable" war.

Daniel Ellsberg has struggled to come to terms with the moral lessons of the Vietnam War. He is clear: The war would have been just as wrong if it had been "winnable."

Both men have prodigious intellects. But McNamara remained emotionally bottled up and ethically paralyzed. In contrast, Ellsberg does not evade the past or live in it; he sees every new day as an opportunity to create a better future.

Even now, mass media rarely publicize Ellsberg's views. Perhaps that's because of a shortage of journalistic fortitude in matters of war and peace.

The media's rage toward McNamara these days seems fueled in part by media aversion to self-examination—as if the more that journalists vent their anger at McNamara, the more they can let themselves off the hook.

In recent weeks, you'd get the impression that the American press led the nation's moral revulsion during the war in Vietnam. No way.

Far from crusading against the war, the national media were gung ho for years. In early 1968, a *Boston Globe* survey of 39 major American daily papers found that not one had taken an editorial position in favor of U.S. withdrawal from Vietnam.

After U.S. soldiers massacred 300 Vietnamese civilians at My Lai in March 1968, nearly a dozen major print and TV outlets suppressed the evidence and photos of the bloodbath for well over a year—until a small, independent news service released the information.

In fact, the mass media always lagged way behind the antiwar stirrings in the American public. The mainstream media's hawks and doves had tactical differences, but neither questioned the right of the U.S. government to carry out aggression against Vietnam 8,000 miles away.

Often credited with getting the U.S. out of Vietnam, network television actually avoided realistic footage of the war—while routinely hyping official pronouncements. "Television coverage did not become substantially more sober until the public, Washington officials and the soldiers in the field had already lost confidence that the war could be won," says scholar Daniel C. Hallin.

This month, the media outrage in response to McNamara's book has largely accepted a key premise that made the press so supportive of escalating the Vietnam War in the first place: *If the war could be won it should be fought*. Pundits are now furious that McNamara knew the war couldn't be won and didn't say so at the time.

Apparently, this country hasn't advanced to the point where— winnable or not—the Vietnam War is seen as wrong, wrong, wrong. No wonder the news media are giving us so much from Robert McNamara, and so little from Daniel Ellsberg.

April 19, 1995

25 Years Since Pentagon Papers: A Dismal Record

A quarter of a century ago, the First Amendment took a deep breath. On June 13, 1971, portions of secret documents appeared in the *New York Times*—and a federal court swiftly issued a restraining order. The *Washington Post* grabbed the baton of press freedom and ran with more excerpts. Weeks later, both newspapers—and the American people—won a momentous victory when the Supreme Court ruled in their favor.

Many were thrilled to see the Nixon administration lose its bid to suppress the Pentagon Papers, which illuminated the U.S. government's nonstop lies about the Vietnam War. For a decade, news media had done much to propagate those lies. But in 1971, with antiwar opinion widespread, newspaper editors moved to expose a history of falsehoods.

Today, it would be pleasant to look back on publication of the Pentagon Papers as a turning point for media coverage of the U.S. military. However, instead of carrying forward the honorable legacy of the Pentagon Papers battle, America's most powerful news outlets have waved the journalistic white flag.

When the U.S. government set out to invade Grenada in 1983 and Panama in 1989, major media echoed the official themes. In autumn 1990, the deployment of U.S. troops to the Persian Gulf paralleled a pre-war media buildup. While the British press debunked White House claims that the purpose was to defend Saudi Arabia, the media spin was very different in the United States.

For the man who'd given the Pentagon Papers to the press, the fall of 1990 felt an awful lot like the fall of 1964. "I was just appalled," Daniel Ellsberg told us a few days ago. "The American newspapers seemed as willing to collaborate in this hoax—this approach to war being carried on covertly—as they had been 25 years earlier, when I was in the Pentagon making plans for the bombing of North Vietnam."

Ironically, Ellsberg singled out two of the worst 1990 offenders: the *New York Times* and the *Washington Post*.

As soon as the first American missiles hit Baghdad in early 1991, mass media leapt into a cheerleading frenzy. With Iraqis — many of them civilians—dying at a rate of thousands per day, news accounts were upbeat. Sanitized phrases like "collateral damage" referred to people perishing under American fire power.

"We lie by not telling you things," a Pentagon official commented to *Newsday* in a moment of candor. That's where journalism is supposed to come in—telling the public what the government wants to keep under wraps.

A few Sundays ago, the symbolism was acute when a ceremony at Arlington National Cemetery unveiled a small memorial for 21 American soldiers who died in secret combat during the 1980s. Back then, the American public remained unaware that U.S. troops were fighting guerrillas in the countryside of El Salvador—where a total of several thousand American servicemen, 55 at a time, played key combat roles such as calling in deadly air strikes.

For most media, the ceremony at Arlington was a time-warp curiosity. Even the better coverage was severely flawed. On CBS, *60 Minutes* aired a May 26 segment that lauded the honor of the U.S. soldiers who'd been deprived of combat ribbons—and ignored the Salvadoran people deprived of their lives.

One of the intrepid journalists who managed to uncover Central American realities, Robert Parry, worked for the Associated Press and *Newsweek* as the 1980s unfolded. He recalls that "editors and bureau chiefs in Washington were far too easily seduced by slick government propagandists, too willing to accept the smear campaigns directed against honest reporters."

Truth is the first casualty of war, but it need not be a fatality.

"If the American people knew that their tax dollars were being used to arm brutal armies which were butchering political dissidents, killing children and raping young girls, then support for the Reagan-Bush policies would have evaporated," Parry says. "With a few notable exceptions, the Washington news media went merrily along with the lies."

Sadly, not much has changed.

June 5, 1996

Nothing Vague About FBI Abuse: Here Are the Dossiers

As the White House pushes to expand FBI powers, some press reports are sounding cautionary notes—usually vague allusions to the FBI's history of harassing political groups and movements.

Missing from most accounts are specifics. This column offers a few of the many horrifying details.

Although President Clinton says stepped-up FBI infiltration will help prevent violence, the record shows that FBI spying has actually abetted violence.

- DICK GREGORY: In 1968, the activist/comedian publicly denounced the Mafia for importing heroin into the inner city. Did the FBI welcome the anti-drug, anti-mob message? No. Head G-man J. Edgar Hoover responded by proposing that the Bureau try to provoke the mob to retaliate against Gregory as part of an FBI "counter intelligence operation" to "neutralize" the comedian. Hoover wrote: "Alert La Cosa Nostra (LCN) to Gregory's attack on LCN."

- FREEDOM RIDERS: In 1961, black and white civil rights workers boarded interstate buses in the North and headed south in an effort to desegregate buses nationwide. The FBI learned that when the freedom riders reached bus depots in Alabama, the state police were going to give the Ku Klux Klan "15 uninterrupted minutes" to beat activists with baseball bats, clubs and chains. The Bureau allowed the violence to occur; activist Walter Bergman spent the rest of his life in a wheelchair, partially paralyzed.

- VIOLA LIUZZO: The white civil rights volunteer from Detroit—a mother of five—joined Martin Luther King's 1965 Selma (Ala.) campaign aimed at securing the right to vote for blacks. She was shot and killed after being chased

20 miles at high speed by a carload of four Klansmen. In the car was Gary David Rowe, a well-paid FBI informant inside the Klan; the violence-prone Rowe had played a big role in the beatings of freedom riders years earlier. "He couldn't be an angel and be a good informant," commented one of his FBI handlers.

- FRANK WILKINSON: A lifelong civil libertarian who led the campaign to abolish the House Committee on Un-American Activities, his FBI surveillance file spans 30 years and 132,000 pages. Estimated cost to us taxpayers: $17 million. Wilkinson never advocated or committed violence, but the file shows that the Bureau burglarized his offices and encouraged beatings of him. The FBI once heard of a right-wing scheme to assassinate Wilkinson—but took no action to inform him or protect him.

- MARTIN LUTHER KING: For years, the FBI used spying and infiltration in a relentless campaign to destroy King— to wreck his marriage, undermine his mental stability and encourage him to commit suicide. The Bureau created dissension among King's associates, disrupted fundraising efforts and recruited his bookkeeper as a paid agent after learning the employee was embezzling.

The FBI utilized "media assets" to plant smear stories in the press—some insinuating that King was a Soviet agent. One FBI media asset against King in the early 1960s was Patrick Buchanan, then an editorial writer in St. Louis.

The FBI once hatched a scheme to "completely discredit" King and have him replaced by a civil rights leader the Bureau could control. The one individual named by the Bureau as "the right kind of Negro leader" was lawyer Samuel Pierce—who years later became the only black in President Reagan's cabinet.

King was hated and regularly threatened by white supremacists and extremists—but the FBI developed a written policy of *not* informing King about threats to his life. Why? Because of his "unsavory character," "arrogance" and "uncooperative attitude."

- PETER BOHMER: For months in the early 1970s, this economics professor and other antiwar activists in San Diego were terrorized—with menacing phone calls, death threats and fire-bombings—by the Secret Army Organization, a right-wing paramilitary group. On Jan. 6, 1972, gunshots were fired into Bohmer's house, wounding a friend.

After a bombing months later, a trial revealed that Howard Barry Godfrey, co-founder of SAO in San Diego and one of its most active and violent members, had all along been a paid FBI informant. Godfrey testified that he had driven the car from which the shots were fired; afterward, he took the weapon to his FBI supervisor, who hid it.

- BLACK PANTHER PARTY: Some critics are denouncing the new movie *Panther* as an anti-FBI fantasy. But the hard facts about the FBI's war on the Panthers were published in 1976 by the Senate Intelligence Committee chaired by Frank Church. Using paid infiltrators and faked documents, the Bureau routinely tried to goad militant groups or street gangs to commit violence against the Panthers.

In southern California, FBI agents helped provoke Ron Karenga's militant US group into attacks on Panthers and boasted about it in memos to headquarters. When the FBI learned that the Panthers and US were trying to talk out their differences, agents did their best to reopen the conflict. Four Panthers were ultimately killed by US members, two on the UCLA campus.

In Chicago, the FBI office forged and sent a letter to the Blackstone Rangers gang leader saying the Panthers had a "hit out" on him. The FBI's stated hope was that he "take reprisals against" the Panther leadership.

Although that plan failed, Chicago Panther chief Fred Hampton (age 21) was killed months later in a predawn police assault on his apartment. Hampton's bodyguard turned out to be an FBI agent-provocateur who, days before the raid, had delivered an apartment floorplan to the Bureau—with an "X" marking Hampton's bed. Most bullets were aimed at his bedroom. The infiltrator received a $300 bonus: "Our source was the man who made the raid possible," stated an FBI memo.

Among the hundreds of schemes detailed in FBI memos were plans to contaminate the Panther newspaper's printing room with a noxious chemical; to inject a powerful laxative into fruit served to kids as part of the Panthers' free breakfast program; and to target smear campaigns at various Hollywood celebrities who had come to the Panthers' defense.

- CENTRAL AMERICA ACTIVISTS: Many recent news accounts say that FBI abuse pretty much ended with J. Edgar Hoover's death in 1972, and that the Bureau has been in check since the Justice Department issued new guidelines in 1976. Not true. FBI disruption of lawful dissent has continued—though the terminology has changed, from counterintelligence (COINTELPRO) to "counterterrorism."

During the 1980s, groups critical of U.S. intervention in Central America were surveilled, infiltrated and disrupted by the FBI. Political break-ins occurred at churches, offices and homes—and material from the burglaries ended up in FBI files. In the guise of monitoring supporters of foreign terrorists, the FBI compiled files on clergy, religious groups and thousands of nonviolent anti-intervention activists. The investigation produced not a single criminal charge. The whole sordid story is detailed in *Break-ins, Death Threats and the FBI*, a book by former *Boston Globe* reporter Ross Gelbspan.

At the center of this spying was FBI official Oliver "Buck" Revell. Today, Revell (now retired) makes the rounds of TV news shows, complaining that the FBI is too hamstrung to track terrorists.

The truth is that the FBI has always had the power to infiltrate terrorist groups. The problem has been the Bureau's diversion of resources to monitor and harass activists whose only "crime" was working for social change.

May 10, 1995

Newest Myth:
"Filegate" Equals Watergate

Repeated incessantly in the echo chamber of conservative punditry, a myth can be fabricated and marketed nationwide almost overnight.

It happened recently when millions of Americans were bombarded with the latest fable: "Filegate" is equivalent to Watergate.

Behind the comparison is a purported "fact" perpetually served up: that the two Clinton employees who obtained FBI files committed the same crime as Watergate convict Charles Colson.

- *The myth is launched.* Cal Thomas started it all in his June 19 [1996] syndicated column, which featured an interview with Colson, self-described "born-again Christian" who used to describe himself as Nixon's chief "hatchet man."

  It seemed as if the old, non-believing, Ninth-Commandment-breaking Colson made a reappearance in Thomas' column. According to Thomas, "Colson called to ask me if I remembered what got him a one-to-three-year prison sentence"—and then Colson provided this answer: "They got me for taking one FBI file and giving it to a reporter."

  Colson went on to express indignation over the "brazen" and "frightening" Clinton administration staffers who obtained the FBI files. "People ought to be marching in the streets over that," said the former foe of street protests.

- *The myth gathers steam.* Tony Snow picked up the thread— half of it, at least—in his syndicated column the next day: "Columnist Cal Thomas notes that Charles Colson got a prison sentence for obtaining one FBI file." No mention of Colson disseminating any files.

- *The myth rockets across the country*, propelled by dozens of media voices. "Does anybody know why Chuck Colson went to jail?" bellowed talk show behemoth Rush Limbaugh. "He looked at unauthorized FBI files.... It's in the latest Cal Thomas column. Colson's reminding everyone that he went to jail for what's going on in Washington today."

On *Larry King Live*, Newt Gingrich asserted that Colson "went to jail for having one file." *Washington Times* editor Wes Pruden declared that Colson "went to prison for the possession of a single FBI file." Wrote the senior columnist for the *Dallas Morning News*: "Tricky Dick Nixon's guys did pen time for misusing just one FBI file."

Told enough times, a fairy tale begins to sound almost true. But in fact, the criminal activities that put Colson behind bars involved far more than a single file.

As White House special counsel, Colson was one of Nixon's closest and dirtiest political operatives, a man who'd "walk over his grandmother" to get Nixon re-elected. It was Colson who brought to the White House—and supervised—E. Howard Hunt, the ex-CIA agent behind the break-in at Democratic headquarters in the Watergate complex.

Newsweek wrote in June 1974 of "the omnipresence of [Colson's] fingerprints across the whole range of Watergate scandals."

"Colson would do anything," Nixon said, as recorded on the White House tapes. Soon after presidential candidate George Wallace was shot, Colson and Nixon hatched a failed plan to have Hunt plant Democratic literature inside the gunman's apartment—"to damage McGovern," in Nixon's taped words.

Colson played a big role in compiling the White House "Enemies List" targeting Nixon critics for federal reprisals. Two White House staffers told investigators that Colson once suggested setting fire to the Brookings Institution, a think tank, to hide a search for documents there.

Charles Colson was ultimately indicted for conspiracy in the burglary of Daniel Ellsberg's psychiatrist. Colson was also indicted for conspiracy and obstruction of justice in the cover-up of the Watergate break-in. If convicted at these two trials, he faced years behind bars.

The Watergate special prosecutor was also investigating Colson's role in obtaining or covering up suspicious campaign pledges from corporate interests (ITT in one case, dairy farmers in another) that had received favors from Nixon's White House.

But Colson, the consummate political fixer, was able to stop these indictments and inquiries by cutting a deal with prosecutors (that's when he announced his religious rebirth)—and agreeing to testify against co-conspirators, one of whom was President Nixon.

The deal let Colson plead guilty to a single felony count: "obstruction of justice" in the Ellsberg case by conspiring to disseminate derogatory material about Ellsberg. He ultimately served seven months in prison and was disbarred.

To say that Colson went to prison because he obtained (or misused) one FBI file is like saying the bloody gangster Al Capone went to prison because he was a tax cheat.

Colson was a Watergate criminal of the highest order, and of Nixon's inner circle. Comparing him to today's low-level "Filegate" operatives is inaccurate and absurd.

Even more absurd is the implication that Filegate is on a par with Watergate—a conspiracy that involved burglaries, bribes, spying, wiretaps, forgeries and other serious political crimes.

July 8, 1996

Part XIII
When News Media Serve the CIA

What happens when an investigative journalist points to serious wrongdoing by a branch of the U.S. government such as the Central Intelligence Agency? Initially, some important information may reach the public. But the responses of top national media outlets are likely to obscure rather than illuminate.

Snow Job:
Establishment Newspapers
Do Damage Control for the CIA

[One of the biggest media uproars of the mid-1990s had to do with the CIA, the Nicaraguan contras and cocaine. As 1997 began, FAIR's magazine *EXTRA!* published an in-depth analysis of how three powerful newspapers handled the controversy. The following "Snow Job" report, written by Norman Solomon, drew on the findings of a FAIR research/reporting team that included Jeff Cohen, Jim Naureckas and Steve Rendall.]

The process has to be conscious, or it would not be carried out with sufficient precision, but it also has to be unconscious, or it would bring with it a feeling of falsity and hence of guilt.... To tell deliberate lies while genuinely believing in them, to forget any fact that has become inconvenient, and then, when it becomes necessary again, to draw it back from oblivion for just so long as it is needed, to deny the existence of objective reality and all the while to take account of the reality which one denies—all this is indispensably necessary.

—*George Orwell*, 1984

For several weeks after an August [1996] series in the *San Jose Mercury News* linked the CIA-backed Nicaraguan contras with the importation of cocaine into poor black areas of Los Angeles, major news outlets did scant reporting on the story. But in early autumn, near-silence gave way to a roar from the country's three most influential urban dailies—the *Washington Post*, *New York Times* and *Los Angeles Times*—which is still reverberating in the national media's echo chamber.

The first *New York Times* article on the subject (9/21/96) foreshadowed much that was to follow. Headlined "Inquiry Is Ordered Into Reports of Contra Cocaine Sales in U.S.," the news story focused on assurances from Central Intelligence Agency director John Deutch and unnamed "former senior CIA officials" that the *Mercury News* assertions were groundless. "I regard these allegations with the utmost seriousness," Deutch said. "They go to the heart and integrity of the CIA enterprise."

Not only did Deutch contend that "the agency never had any relationship" with Nicaraguan drug traffickers Oscar Danilo Blandon and Norvin Meneses—the *Times* also reported the reassuring news that "former senior CIA officials involved in the contra operations said this week that they had never heard of" Blandon or Meneses. None of the article's dozen paragraphs included any suggestion that the CIA might be a dubious touchstone for veracity. The notion that the CIA's internal probe held a key to unlocking the story's mysteries was to be oft-repeated.

Yet the uproar over the *Mercury News* series, written by reporter Gary Webb, continued to grow. Denials from the CIA carried little weight with much of the public, particularly African-Americans outraged by the series. Protests mounted in cities from Los Angeles to Washington, and members of the Congressional Black Caucus demanded federal investigations.

October [1996] brought a fierce counterattack from the *Post*, the *New York Times* and *L.A. Times*, all of which published lengthy news articles blasting the *Mercury News* series. In the process, a number of recurrent debunking themes quickly gained the status of media truisms.

"Last month," *Newsweek* reported in November, "the *Merc* started getting trashed—by its peers. In turn, the *Washington Post*, *Los Angeles Times* and *New York Times* poked holes in the story, exhaustively and mercilessly."

In his role as the *Post*'s in-house media critic, Howard Kurtz took numerous swipes at Webb that grew increasingly dismissive; one item, headed "A Webb of Conspiracy," ended with the smug one-liner, "Oliver Stone, check your voice mail." Liberal columnist Mary McGrory, based at the *Post*, echoed what she was hearing all around her in an Oct. 27 piece: "The San Jose story has been discredited by major publications, including the *Post*."

By November, a clear orthodoxy had taken hold. Certain *de rigueur* phrases began appearing in news articles: "Many of the series' conclusions have been widely challenged" (*Washington Post*, 11/6/96); "media critics and other newspapers have questioned the *Mercury News*' findings." (AP in *New York Times*, 11/7/96)

Under the headline "CIA Chief Denies Crack Conspiracy," the *New York Times* (11/16/96) indicated that reputable media outlets—and reputable spooks—had rejected the *Mercury News* series: "Agency officials said they had no evidence of any such plot. Other news organizations were not able to confirm the plot. Still, the rumor mill continued to grind, seemingly unstoppable." The next day, *Times* columnist Maureen Dowd took the company line: "Mr. Deutch and investigators for several major newspapers have found no evidence to support the conspiracy theory that grew out of a series in the *San Jose Mercury News* suggesting a CIA role in the spread of crack in America's inner cities."

Suspect Sources

But what exactly in the *San Jose Mercury News* stories was refuted by these "major newspapers"? To a notable degree, the establishment papers relied for their debunking of the *Mercury News* on the CIA's own obligatory denials. As journalist Marc Cooper pointed out in the weekly *New Times Los Angeles*, "Regarding the all-important question of how much responsibility the CIA had, we are being asked to take the word of *sources* who in a more objective account would be considered *suspects*."

In the *New York Times*' full-page magnum opus on the controversy (10/21/96), reporter Tim Golden drew extensively on interviews with nameless sources such as "government officials with access to intelligence reports," not to mention "more than two dozen current and former [contra] rebels, CIA officials and narcotics agents, as well as other law-enforcement officials and experts on the drug trade." The *Times* seemed eager to take at face value the statements at CIA headquarters that the agency didn't know Blandon from Adam: "Although he claimed to have supplied several thousand pounds of cocaine to one of the biggest crack dealers in Southern California, officials said the CIA had no record of Mr. Blandon before he appeared as a central figure in the series in the *Mercury News*." As in the first *Times* report, featuring the same CIA disclaimers, there was not the slightest hint that such denials might be self-serving.

The *Los Angeles Times* was on the same track in its lengthy three-day series. "CIA officials insist they knew nothing about Meneses' and Blandon's tainted contributions to [Adolfo] Calero or other contra leaders," the newspaper reported (10/21/96). One of the officials quoted in support of the claim that the CIA had drug-free hands was Vincent Cannistraro—identified by the newspaper only as a "former CIA official."

In fact—though the *L.A. Times* could spare none of the article's several thousand words to let readers know—Cannistraro was in charge of the CIA's contra activities during the early 1980s. After moving to the National Security Council in 1984, he became a supervisor of covert aid to Afghanistan's mujahedeen guerrillas, whose involvement in the opium trade made Afghanistan and Pakistan two of the world's main suppliers of heroin. If the *L.A. Times* had been willing to share such relevant details, it would have provided readers with a much better basis for evaluating Cannistraro's testimonial to CIA integrity: "There's no tendency to turn a blind eye to drug trafficking. It's too sensitive. It's not a fine line. It's not a shaded area where you can turn away from the rules."

The *L.A. Times* was following in the footsteps of less august media outlets that used a deceptively identified Cannistraro to attack the *Mercury News* series. The right-wing *Washington Times* quoted him as saying that the series "doesn't have any elements of authenticity." And former *Washington Times* reporter Michael Hedges wrote a Scripps-Howard News Service article that called Cannistraro a "retired CIA counterterrorism and Latin America expert" and quoted him as declaring: "I have personal knowledge that the CIA knew nothing about these guys [Blandon and Meneses]. These charges are completely illogical."

Besides self-serving denials, journalistic critics of the *Mercury News* offered little to rebut the paper's specific pieces of evidence—including Blandon's own testimony and law enforcement documents and comments—indicating that Meneses and Blandon may have been protected by federal agents.

Whose Army?

Judging the *Mercury News* series invalid, the pre-eminent denouncers frequently berated the newspaper for failing to prove what Webb never claimed. The *Washington Post*, for instance, devoted paragraph after paragraph of its Oct. 4 barrage to illuminating what Webb had already acknowledged in his articles—that while he proves contra links to major cocaine importation, he can't identify specific CIA officials who knew of or condoned the trafficking.

Many critics took issue with Webb's references to the contras as "the CIA's army." The *Washington Post*'s Kurtz, for example, complained that "Webb's repeated use of the phrase 'the CIA's army'...clearly suggests that the agency was involved."

In fact, referring to the Nicaraguan Democratic Force (FDN) as the CIA's army is solid journalism, highlighting a relationship that is fundamentally relevant to the story. The army was formed at the instigation of the CIA, its leaders were selected by and received salaries from the agency, and CIA officers controlled day-to-day battlefield strategies. One former contra leader, Edgar Chamorro, has said that the FDN's leaders were "nothing more than the executioners of the CIA's orders."

Yet the newsroom culture of denial grew so strong that a *Washington Post* article in November, by Marc Fisher, seemed to dispute that the CIA and the contras had any ties at all: "On WRC, [talkshow host] Joe Madison droned on as he has for weeks about the supposed CIA-contra connection."

In its big blast at the *Mercury News* series, the *New York Times* tried a semantic maneuver to distance the CIA's army from the CIA. The newspaper acknowledged that Meneses and Blandon "traveled once to Honduras to see the FDN's military commander, Enrique Bermudez." But the *Times* quickly added: "Although Mr. Bermudez, like other contra leaders, was often paid by the CIA, he was not a CIA agent."

It was classic sleight-of-hand at the keyboard, as *Newsday* columnist Murray Kempton pointed out: "The maintenance of such distinctions without any essential difference is one of the more cunning of the infinite devices the agency employs on obfuscation. The CIA identifies highly placed foreign hirelings not as 'agents' but as 'assets.'" Just such obfuscation helped many journalists to assert that the *Mercury News* series had been debunked and that the CIA was unfairly implicated.

Dubious Debunkings

The most potentially damaging charge made by the establishment papers is that Webb greatly exaggerated the amount of crack profits going to the contras, which he reported as being "millions" of dollars. "According to law enforcement officials, Blandon sold $30,000 to $60,000 worth of cocaine in two transactions and delivered the money to Meneses for shipment to the contras," the *Washington Post* reported. "Meneses was indeed a financial contributor to the contras," the *L.A. Times* reported, "but his donations to the rebel cause amounted to no more than $50,000, according to two men who knew him at the time." These estimates quickly became enshrined as journalistic fact. They were even given credence by an editorial in *The Nation*: Blandon and Meneses' contributions to the contra cause "may have been $50,000," David Corn wrote.

Yet the *Mercury News'* higher estimates are better sourced than the debunkers' low numbers. In contrast to the *Mercury News*—which had drawn on sworn grand jury and court testimony to calculate that millions of crack dollars flowed to the contras—the *Post* and *L.A. Times* attributed their much smaller estimates to unnamed sources, variously described as "law enforcement officials" (*Washington Post*, 10/4/96), "a contra supporter and a business partner who sold drugs with Blandon" (*L.A. Times*, 10/20/96) and "associates in drug trafficking in Los Angeles" (*L.A. Times*, 10/21/96).

Nor do the claims by the *Washington Post* and *New York Times* stand up that the funneling of crack money to the contras ended early in the 1980s. Pete Carey, a reporter assigned by the *Mercury News* to do a reassessment of the paper's own reporting (10/13/96), presented fuller documentation: "A 1986 Los Angeles County sheriff's affidavit for searches of the homes and business

That Delusional Mindset

Noting that "both the *Washington Post* and the *Los Angeles Times* have taken a look at the allegations and found them baseless," *Washington Post* columnist Richard Cohen (10/24/96) went on to label the CIA-contra-crack story "literally incredible—although not all that different from Louis Farrakhan's insistence that AIDS is somehow spread or induced by the government." Dispensing with any semblance of nuance, Cohen was blaring a popular media theme: The *San Jose Mercury News* series had fallen on the fertile ground of African-American propensities for paranoia. "A piece of black America remains hospitable to the most bizarre rumors and myths—the one about the CIA and crack being just one," Cohen wrote.

Richard Cohen was one of many journalists depicting anger at CIA-cocaine links as a byproduct of black paranoia. *Time* (9/30/96) got the ball rolling nationwide with a piece by Jack E. White, who provided gratuitous asides about "conspiracy theories" and "bizarre fantasies." That approach quickly became a stylish media fixation—reducing documented allegations against the CIA to the level of sociological curiosities.

This theme of black paranoia accompanied all three of the major papers' attacks on the *Mercury News* series. Often the coverage dripped with condescension, as when the *Washington Post*'s Hamil R. Harris (10/24/96) scolded a mostly black audience for not giving credence to CIA denials: "It didn't matter to the crowd that CIA inspector general Frederick P. Hitz told the panel that a brief 1988 study concluded 'the agency neither participated in nor condoned drug trafficking by the contra forces.' Most in the crowd decided not to believe him a long time ago."

Media wonderment over African-Americans' strange beliefs reached a high pitch of unintended irony in Tim Golden's Oct. 21 [1996] *New York Times* report. Golden noted that "in 1990, long before any major news organizations had connected crack and the CIA," a poll showed that many blacks already believed that the government deliberately allowed drugs into the black community. Talk about bizarre fantasies: 1990 was years after a number of major news organizations, including the Associated Press (12/20/85) and CBS News (*West 57th*, 4/6/87, 7/11/87), documented involvement by the CIA-backed contras in the cocaine trade—not to mention the documentation of CIA participation in opium trafficking in Southeast Asia (*The Politics of Heroin*, Alfred W. McCoy). The mainstream media's ability to simply ignore any evidence that doesn't fit their worldview is the true mark of the delusional mindset.

of Blandon and members of his drug ring shows that the contra connection lasted into the mid-1980s. In the 1986 affidavit, three confidential informants said that Blandon was still sending money to the contras."

The establishment papers' orthodoxy also insists that "Freeway" Ricky Ross, the contact who distributed Blandon's cocaine in the form of crack, was not a key player in the drug's proliferation. The *Washington Post* declared that Ross' activities were incidental to the spread of crack; using identical language in a pair of news articles (10/4/96, 10/12/96), the Post insisted that available data "point to the rise of crack as a broad-based phenomenon driven in numerous places by players of different nationalities." The *New York Times* concluded rather cryptically that "several experts on the drug trade said that although Mr. Ross was indeed a crack kingpin, he was one of many."

But two years earlier—before the public learned that much of his cocaine was supplied by smugglers connected to the contras—the same man was the subject of a 2,400-word *Los Angeles Times* news article (12/20/94) that portrayed him as central to the spread of crack cocaine. "If there was an eye to the storm," the article began, "if there was a criminal mastermind behind crack's decade-long reign, if there was one outlaw capitalist most responsible for flooding Los Angeles' streets with mass-marketed cocaine, his name was Freeway Rick." The headline? "Deposed King of Crack; Now Free After 5 Years in Prison, This Master Marketer Was Key to the Drug's Spread in L.A."

The article reported that as far as crack went, "Ross did more than anyone else to democratize it, boosting volume, slashing prices and spreading disease on a scale never before conceived." He became "South-Central's first millionaire crack lord," the newspaper reported. "While most other dealers toiled at the bottom rungs of the market, his coast-to-coast conglomerate was selling more than 500,000 rocks a day, a staggering turnover that put the drug within reach of anyone with a few dollars."

In a remarkable display of subservience to prevailing orthodoxy, the same reporter who wrote those words, Jesse Katz, went on to write a front-page article for the *L.A. Times* (10/20/96) that reads like a show-trial recantation. Ross now was one of many "interchangeable characters," who was "dwarfed" by other dealers. "How the crack epidemic reached that extreme, on some level, had nothing to do with Ross," Katz reported. The *L.A.Times* reporter did not explain how his reporting on Ross two years earlier could have been so inaccurate.

Evidence Ignored

While the *Mercury News* series could arguably be faulted for occasional overstatement, the elite media's attacks on the series were clearly driven by a need to defend their shoddy record on the contra-cocaine story—involving a decade-long suppression of evidence. The *Washington Post* was typical. "When Brian Barger and I wrote the first story about contra-cocaine smuggling for the Associated Press in December 1985," Robert Parry recalls, "the *Post* waited a week, added some fresh denials and then stuck the story near the back of the national news section."

In July 1987, the House Narcotics Committee, chaired by Rep. Charles Rangel (D-N.Y.), investigated contra-drug allegations and found a "need for further congressional investigation." The *Washington Post* distorted reality with the headline "Hill Panel Finds No Evidence Linking Contras to Drug Smuggling"— and then refused to publish Rangel's letter correcting the record.

Later that year, *Time* magazine staff writer Laurence Zuckerman was assigned to work with an investigative reporter on contra-cocaine allegations. They found serious evidence of the link, but the story Zuckerman wrote was obstructed by higher-ups. A senior editor acknowledged to Zuckerman: "*Time* is institutionally behind the contras. If this story were about the Sandinistas and drugs, you'd have no trouble getting it in the magazine."

Two years later, the Senate subcommittee chaired by John Kerry released a scathing condemnation of U.S. government complicity with narcotics trafficking by or for the contras. Among Kerry's conclusions: "Individuals who provided support for the contras were involved in drug trafficking, the supply network of the contras was used by drug trafficking organizations, and elements of the contras themselves knowingly received financial and material assistance from drug traffickers. In each case, one or another agency of the U.S. government had information regarding the involvement either while it was occurring, or immediately thereafter."

Parry remembers the reaction: "When this important report was issued in April 1989, the *Post* buried the information in a scant 700-word article on page A20. And most of that story, by Michael Isikoff, was devoted to Republican criticisms of Kerry, rather than to the serious evidence of contra wrongdoing. Other establishment publications took the cue that it was safe to mock Kerry. *Newsweek* dubbed him a 'randy conspiracy buff.'"

In July 1989, former White House operative Oliver North, National Security Adviser John Poindexter, U.S. ambassador to Costa Rica Lewis Tambs, CIA station chief Joseph Fernandez and other contragate figures were barred from Costa Rica—on orders of that country's president, Oscar Arias, who acted on recommendations from a Costa Rican congressional commission investigating drug trafficking. The commission concluded that the contra resupply network in Costa Rica, which North coordinated from the White House, doubled as a drug smuggling operation.

A big story? Not at all. Although AP sent out a dispatch, the *New York Times* and the three major TV networks failed to mention it; the *Washington Post* ran the news as a short back-page item. When FAIR's Steve Rendall called the *Post* to find out why, reporter Walter Pincus—who later co-wrote the *Post*'s 1996 attack on the *San Jose Mercury News*—made no apologies. "Just because a congressional commission in Costa Rica says something, doesn't mean it's true," Pincus said (*EXTRA!*, 10-11/89).

In late 1996, one of the basic pretensions threading through much of the coverage by the *Washington Post, New York Times* and *L.A. Times* was the notion that contra participation in drug trafficking is old news—a particularly ironic claim coming from newspapers that went out of their way to ignore or disparage key information during the 1980s. The *Post*'s ombudsman, Geneva Overholser, was on target (11/10/96) when she re-raised the question of the U.S. government's relationship to drug smuggling and noted that the three newspapers "showed more passion for sniffing out the flaws in San Jose's answer than for sniffing out a better answer themselves."

Citing "strong previous evidence that the CIA at least chose to overlook contra involvement in the drug trade," Overholser found "misdirected zeal" in the *Post*'s response to the *Mercury News* series: "Would that we had welcomed the surge of public interest as an occasion to return to a subject the *Post* and the public had given short shrift. Alas, dismissing someone else's story as old news comes more naturally." A more pointed observation came from Robert Parry: The irony of the *Post*'s big Oct. 4 story "was that the newspaper was finally accepting the reality of contra cocaine trafficking, albeit in a backhanded way." The *Post* "had long pooh-poohed earlier allegations that the contras were implicated in drug shipments."

Our Man at the *Post*

Walter Pincus, the *Washington Post*'s lead reporter in taking on the *San Jose Mercury News* series linking the contras to the crack epidemic, is on record as a believer in agencies like the CIA. At a forum in spring 1995, Pincus told the audience: "You never should and never will get rid of intelligence organizations."

Pincus' bio says that he "served in the U.S. Army Counterintelligence Corps, stationed in Washington," from 1955 to 1957, and went on to become "Washington correspondent for three North Carolina newspapers" in 1959. What his bio doesn't mention is that in 1960, he was recruited by CIA employees to serve as a U.S. representative at two international conferences—his trips paid for by CIA fronts. Pincus was unapologetic when he disclosed his CIA role in a 1967 piece he wrote soon after joining the staff of the *Washington Post*. (Ironically, that *Post* article was reprinted in the *San Jose Mercury*, 2/18/67.)

In July 1996, the *Washington Times*, a newspaper that hardly considers affinity with the CIA to be a reportorial sin, described Pincus as a journalist "who some in the agency refer to as 'the CIA's house reporter.'"

A Dirty, Dangerous World

What explains these elite media outlets' shameful record of suppressing evidence that the CIA's contra army was involved in the drug trade—and attacking those who dared to report the story?

In the case of the *New York Times* and the *Washington Post*, part of the explanation is that the papers had lent their editorial prestige to the contra cause. By the late 1980s, both papers had endorsed military aid to the contras—though sometimes grudgingly. In February 1988, a pair of pro-contra aid *Post* editorials bracketed a crucial vote in Congress; the pre-vote editorial observed approvingly that "a carrot-and-stick combination has moved the Sandinistas." There was no discernible concern that the military "stick" was being used to take the lives of civilian peasants in the Nicaraguan countryside.

At all three papers, the attitudes of owners and top management set the tone and impose the constraints within which journalists work. Dennis McDougal, a former *L.A. Times* staffer, described the paper's editor, Shelby Coffey III, this way: "He is the dictionary definition of someone who wants to protect the status quo. He weighs whether or not an investigative piece will have repercussions among the ruling elite, and if it will, the chances of seeing it in print in the *L.A. Times* decrease accordingly."

The *New York Times* and *Washington Post* have an even closer relationship to the nation's elites, with connections to the CIA that go back nearly to the agency's founding. In a piece on the CIA and news media written for *Rolling Stone* two decades ago (10/20/77), Watergate reporter Carl Bernstein wrote that "the agency's relationship with the [*New York*] *Times* was by far its most valuable among newspapers, according to CIA officials. From 1950 to 1966, about 10 CIA employees were provided *Times* cover under arrangements approved by the newspaper's late publisher, Arthur Hays Sulzberger. The cover arrangements were part of a general *Times* policy—set by Sulzberger—to provide assistance to the CIA whenever possible."

Bernstein's former employer, the *Washington Post*, was also useful to the CIA; Bernstein quoted a CIA official as saying of the

Post's late owner and publisher, "It was widely known that Phil Graham was somebody you could get help from."

Descendants of these publishers still run their respective papers, and the attitude that they have an obligation to provide covert help to the CIA persists to the present era. In 1988, *Post* owner Katharine Graham, Phil's widow, gave a speech at the CIA's Langley, Va. headquarters. "We live in a dirty and dangerous world," Graham told agency leaders. "There are some things the general public does not need to know and shouldn't. I believe democracy flourishes when the government can take legitimate steps to keep its secrets and when the press can decide whether to print what it knows."

Readers, in turn, can decide how much faith to put in news outlets whose owners embrace such a philosophy.

Part XIV
Human Rights,
Media Wrongs

In many countries, political imprisonments combine with violence and torture to maintain an atmosphere that is intimidating if not terrifying. We hear about human-rights violations overseas, but the reporting is often quite selective.

Human Rights:
The Incomplete Story

The man who won the presidency 20 years ago called human rights "the soul of our foreign policy." Jimmy Carter liked to talk about human rights. In sharp contrast, during the 1996 campaign, Bill Clinton and Bob Dole have reinforced the prevailing media judgment: Human rights aren't very important.

Around the globe, it's no secret that Washington is more concerned about economic markets and geopolitical clout than human rights. Many regimes enjoy good relations with the White House while using brutal repression to crush dissent.

Here at home, we're in a vicious cycle: Politicians say little on the subject of human rights. Journalists don't perceive it as a key issue. Politicians don't see much press coverage and figure they can skip it.

What's lacking is vigilant— and independent—media attention to human rights all over the world. While political jailings and torture are widespread, American editors and reporters are inclined to take their cues from top U.S. officials.

If the president or secretary of state condemns a particular nation for human-rights violations, the media focus is likely to be extensive. So, for instance, we've learned plenty about horrible abuses in Iraq. But we don't hear much about the documented torture in bordering countries that are longtime U.S. allies — Turkey and Saudi Arabia.

Some news accounts are exceptional. But a story needs amplification to make a big noise. If other media fail to follow up, there's no "echo effect," and the unusual reporting doesn't make a lot of difference.

A human-rights story gets more editorial mileage when it "coincides with the dominant 'spin' from Washington," according to Human Rights Watch staffer Joe Stork. And on the tube, "aside from major atrocity stories such as the genocidal campaigns in

Rwanda and Bosnia, human rights seldom makes the TV-news sound bite."

In fact, television's foreign news is dwindling. "Overseas coverage has declined on the networks by some 50 percent over the last 10 years," says veteran TV news producer Danny Schechter. Solid reports on human rights are "episodic," he told us.

Since 1993, Schechter and partner Rory O'Connor at Globalvision have bucked the trend by producing the public-TV program *Rights & Wrongs*. No distribution help has come from the national PBS system—run by executives who "never backed away from their statement that human rights is an 'insufficient organizing principle' for a TV series," Schechter notes. "They made that statement before we even produced the series."

Resisting the arrogance at PBS headquarters, *Rights & Wrongs* airs on 140 stations; viewers get journalism from across the globe. Funded by foundations and the Independent Television Service, *Rights & Wrongs* is battling to challenge media complacency.

Every day, news blips go by us without any reference to the human-rights implications. That's what happened last month, when the Clinton adminstration confirmed plans to sell nine F-16 fighter jets to Indonesia's dictatorship.

Now, the 1996 Nobel Peace Prize has gone to a Catholic bishop and an exiled activist who've been part of the long struggle for human rights in East Timor—a country occupied by Indonesian troops since 1975. In a way, the award also serves as a belated booby prize for Jimmy Carter and mainstream media.

Inaugurated in January 1977—just 13 months after Indonesia launched its bloody invasion of East Timor—President Carter stepped up U.S. shipments of weaponry to the Jakarta regime as it continued with wholesale murder of Timorese civilians. Before Carter left the White House, the death toll reached an estimated 200,000 people, nearly a third of the entire population of East Timor.

Dazzled by Carter's idealistic rhetoric, American news media ignored those grisly realities—and, for two decades, paid very little attention to the torture and slaughter of Timorese people.

Clearly, we need much more than a return to human-rights platitudes from the White House.

October 16, 1996

School of the Terrorists...
Near CNN Headquarters in Atlanta

Most Americans abhor nations that promote terrorism. We'd be outraged to hear that some country actually maintains a school for many of the world's top kidnappers, torturers and assassins.

If such a school existed, and if it were the subject of intense scrutiny on network TV, it's easy to imagine thousands of aroused citizens demanding that Washington take action to shut the school down.

In fact, such a school does exist. Only it's not on foreign soil. And Washington has not shut it down; Congress keeps it open—with millions of taxpayer dollars yearly.

The U.S. Army's school is located at Fort Benning, Georgia. It's called the School of the Americas, but in Latin America it's known by other names: School of the Assassins; School of the Dictators; School of the Coups.

The school has been mentioned in the news recently because Guatemalan Col. Julio Alpirez—a CIA operative—was implicated in two crimes: the 1990 murder of a U.S. citizen who ran an inn in Guatemala, and the 1992 torture and murder of a Guatemalan leftist guerrilla leader married to an American lawyer.

Col. Alpirez is an alumnus of the School of the Americas. He studied there as a young soldier in 1970, and again 20 years later, when he completed graduate training for senior military officers. A few months after that, Alpirez directed the murder of the American innkeeper.

Alpirez is a small-fry thug compared to some of SOA's other graduates, who include Panama's former dictator Gen. Manuel Noriega and Salvadoran mass murderer Roberto D'Aubuisson.

Listen to the U.S. Army personnel in charge of SOA describe its mission, and you hear rhetoric about training military leaders from Latin America and the Caribbean in democracy and human rights. But action speaks louder than words.

In 1988, the first graduate inducted into SOA's "Hall of Fame" was former Bolivian dictator Hugo Banzer, who seized power in a violent 1971 military coup and brutally suppressed dissent for years.

Other Hall of Famers include Gen. Manuel Antonio Callejas, a Guatemalan intelligence chief who presided over the deaths of thousands; Gen. Policarpio Paz Garcia, a corrupt Honduran dictator; and drug-trafficking suspect Humberto Regalado Hernandez, a Honduran general who took four separate courses at the school.

Framed pictures of these men are proudly displayed in SOA's main foyer. If these are SOA's Hall of Famers, we wonder who's in its Hall of Shame.

"American faculty members readily accepted all forms of military dictatorship in Latin America," asserts Joseph Blair, a U.S. Army instructor at the school from 1986 to 1989.

Occasionally, armies in Latin America have battled each other in border wars. But mostly, they do battle against their own people—especially the poor, peasant groups and labor unions, priests and church activists who work for human rights.

SOA is right in the middle of these dirty wars. Each year, it instructs 2,000 soldiers from the region in counterinsurgency, intelligence, interrogation and psychological warfare.

Martin Almada, a well-known political prisoner under Paraguay's military regime, was researching his own case in that country's "Horror Archives" when he found materials labeled *Instruction at the School of Americas*. They included a torture manual that instructed "interrogators" on how to keep electric-shock victims alive for further questioning.

In 1993, the United Nations released its detailed "Truth Commission Report on El Salvador," identifying the men responsible for atrocities against civilians during the decade-long civil war. Most of the culprits in the major murders were SOA graduates.

Two of the three military officers cited for assassinating Salvadoran Archbishop Oscar Romero in 1980 were SOA graduates. So were three of the five officers involved in the rape and murder of four U.S. church women who worked with Salvador's poor; 10 of 12 officers involved in the El Mozote massacre, which left hundreds of unarmed peasants killed and mutilated; and 19 of 27 officers involved in the massacre of six Jesuit priests, their cook and her daughter on a university campus in 1989.

While the war against Latin America's poor may benefit U.S.-based corporations with plantations or factories in the region, it brings only disgrace to the U.S. citizenry as a whole. Yet we taxpayers heavily fund that war, in part through SOA.

At Fort Benning, Col. Alpirez and others who attended the nine-month Command and General Staff College received up to $25,000 in living allowances (in addition to their regular salaries), and free weekend trips to see Atlanta Braves baseball games or Disney World.

When it comes to federal spending, Newt Gingrich is quite vocal. But he doesn't criticize the millions spent on the school of the assassins in his home state.

Last May [1994], Gingrich and others voted 217-175 to defeat a House measure that would have ended funding for the school. The amendment was sponsored by Massachusetts Rep. Joe Kennedy, an individual who knows well the horror of political assassination.

On March 24, 1995—the fifteenth anniversary of Archbishop Romero's murder by SOA graduates—religious activists began a fast at the U.S. Capitol to stop SOA funding. The fast is led by Father Roy Bourgeois of SOA Watch, a Maryknoll priest who has served over two years in prison for his protests against the school.

You might ask why the school—located only about 90 minutes from CNN headquarters in Atlanta—has not been subjected to ongoing, hard-hitting TV coverage. After all, it's got everything network TV seems to want in a story: Blood, gore, terror.

[In September 1996, a brief flurry of press coverage followed the Pentagon's release of documents acknowledging that School of the Americas training manuals throughout the 1980s advocated torture, executions and false imprisonment.]

March 29, 1995

Father Roy Bourgeois, SOA Watch

Beyond Oklahoma City:
A Nation Where Terrorism Rules

In the painful aftermath of the Oklahoma City tragedy, news coverage has gone to great lengths to convey the humanity of victims and the grief of survivors. As a result, the emotional realities of terrorism now seem much more real to Americans.

What would it be like to live in a country where terrorists struck with impunity on a regular basis, matching the Oklahoma death toll every few weeks?

And what if most of the nation's terrorists—rather than reviling the government—were actually *aligned with* the government, or even part of it?

That's the situation in Colombia, where political killings total 4,000 a year, in a South American nation of 33 million people. If a similar proportion of the population were dying from political violence in the United States, that would add up to about 600 people killed by terrorism *every week*.

When U.S. media outlets mention the Colombian carnage, it's usually in stories blaming drug traffickers for the bloodshed. Yet, as journalist Ana Carrigan pointed out this spring [1995] in the NACLA magazine *Report on the Americas*, "the media's single-minded obsession with drugs" has gotten in the way of telling the truth.

Out of 25,491 politically linked killings of noncombatant Colombian civilians during the last eight years, *less than 3 percent* of the murders were related to the drug trade, according to the Andean Commission of Jurists. Twenty-nine percent of the deaths were attributed to left-wing rural guerrillas and urban insurgents.

Contrary to the impression left by U.S. media accounts, Carrigan reports, nearly 70 percent of the political murders with identified perpetrators "have been committed by the Colombian army and police, or by paramilitary groups and privately financed death squads operating in partnership with state forces."

In effect, the partnership extends to Washington—which keeps sending U.S. taxpayers' money to the Colombian government, despite its horrendous record:

- Each year, hundreds of Colombian children—many of them poor street kids—are killed by death squads engaged in "social cleansing." Human Rights Watch charges that young people arrested by police are regularly beaten, raped and tortured with electric shocks. Special army units also torture children, viewing them as "potential informants on their parents."

- "Political cleansing" goes on daily. In November 1992, for example, eight children associated with a nonviolent, progressive Christian group were massacred in Medellin. The accused include members of a U.S.-trained police intelligence squad.

- After a skirmish with guerrillas near Trujillo a few years ago, soldiers and police rounded up dozens of suspected civilian "sympathizers" in the town. Their mutilated bodies were later found floating in a river. Some had been burned with blowtorches, others had limbs amputated with a chainsaw.

- Paramilitary groups murdered more than 100 labor unionists in Colombia last year.

The U.S. media's favorite plot line—pitting Colombia's noble authorities against nefarious drug traffickers—fits in well with rationales for U.S. government aid, providing Colombian police with about $18 million annually. In addition, Colombia has been a top Latin American buyer of military equipment from the United States; last year's purchases were in the neighborhood of $73 million.

Nine months ago, Manuel Cepeda—a senator leading the left-wing opposition—was gunned down on a Bogota street. A paramilitary group, calling itself "Death to Communists and Guerrillas," quickly claimed responsibility.

Government investigators have tied the murder to Fidel Castano, a well-known paramilitary chieftain, named on seven current arrest warrants related to massacres. Yet he continues to move freely between Colombia and his apartment in Paris.

In the United States, media attention to Colombia's political violence is sparse—and skewed. "The news coverage is completely inadequate because it always seems to focus on so-called drug-related violence," says Mario Murillo of the Pacifica radio network's New York station WBAI, who has reported frequently from Colombia.

"The U.S. aid is supposedly used, and justified, in the name of combating drugs," Murillo told us. But "a majority of U.S. aid is actually being used to combat the guerrillas and the civilian popular sectors struggling for social change."

Most of the victims of Colombian terrorism are peaceable civilians—brutally murdered as surely as the victims in Oklahoma City. No less than the people we have seen so often on our TV screens in recent weeks, their loved ones are left behind to weep and to mourn. But the circumstances of such grief are off the media map.

May 3, 1995

U.S.-Mexico Military Ties: Unexamined and Growing

When the United States and Mexico went to war 150 years ago, the conflict stirred fierce arguments north of the Rio Grande. Controversy raged as Congress approved a declaration of war on May 13, 1846.

Most newspapers endorsed the war with Mexico. The *New York Herald* claimed, "It is a part of our destiny to civilize that beautiful country." But, in the same city, *Tribune* editor Horace Greeley demanded: "Is not Life miserable enough, comes not Death soon enough, without resort to the hideous enginery of War?"

The Mexican war split the ranks of literary notables as well. Poet Walt Whitman was enthusiastic: "Mexico must be thoroughly chastised!... America knows how to crush, as well as how to expand!" In contrast, Henry David Thoreau protested the war by going to jail rather than paying a poll tax.

Today, far from clashing on the battlefield, the two nations are engaged in extensive military teamwork. The growing martial alliance is not debated in the United States, where few people even know it exists.

News watchers remain in the dark while the U.S. government provides Mexican armed forces with high-tech military equipment and training to suppress Indian peasants. The aid has grave consequences for human rights.

Despite a flurry of news coverage after indigenous Mayans launched an uprising in Mexico's southern state of Chiapas at the start of 1994, the U.S. role has stayed in the shadows.

Yet, in his award-winning book *Rebellion From the Roots*, journalist John Ross cites Bell-212 transport helicopters obtained from the United States: "There is little doubt that the U.S. aircraft was used by the Mexican military to wage war on the Indians of Chiapas." At the outset, Ross writes, those helicopters "were utilized by the military to ferry prisoners and the dead."

When more than 100 Indians died in early January 1994, much of the lethal firepower came from the sky. Two months later, a Zapatista guerrilla leader known as Commandante Humberto told reporters in the town of San Cristobal: "We want the government of the United States to retire its helicopters because they are being used to repress the Mexican people."

But, instead of pulling back from military entanglement, Washington is now plunging ahead. In late April [1996], Defense Secretary William Perry huddled with his Mexican counterpart, Gen. Enrique Cervantes Aguirre, to "explore ways in which our militaries could cooperate better."

The pair worked out an unprecedented deal. This year, the U.S. Department of Defense will give Mexico's air force about 50 helicopters—Hueys—originally developed for combat. Delivery of the first dozen is set for early summer.

Pentagon sources assert that this is the Defense Department's first direct transfer of aircraft to the Mexican military. "For us, it's a very big story, very important," says Jose Carreño, a Washington correspondent for the Mexico City daily *El Universal*. "We have been covering it. For whatever reason, the U.S. news media have not."

In theory, the Huey helicopters will primarily serve Mexico's anti-drug program. In practice, the Mexican command can do whatever it wants with them. "They don't have any strings attached," a top Mexican official explained on April 24. In any event, the copters are sure to strengthen the air power of a government that's still on a war footing with indigenous rebels.

Political bloodshed persists in the Chiapas region, where Indian guerrillas receive wide support from a native population that has endured lifetimes of poverty and racial discrimination— along with violent repression from Mexican police and government troops.

Amnesty International charges that human rights violators commit heinous crimes with "impunity" in Mexico. New documents from Human Rights Watch show that "government officials arbitrarily detained, tortured and forced confessions from suspects" during a crackdown in Chiapas last year. Torture and killings of peaceful protesters also occurred elsewhere in the country.

The latest independent reports make for grisly reading. But perhaps most upsetting is a statement by Human Rights Watch: "As it has in the past, the Clinton administration went out of its way to avoid criticizing the Mexican government on human rights issues."

Apparently, the White House is convinced that few of us will notice its shameful silence—or consider the dire implications as the United States widens its military pipeline into Mexico.

May 1, 1996

Egypt's Media Image
Conceals Grim Realities

When President Clinton visited Egypt a few days ago [in March 1996], the media spotlight fell briefly on a country that receives enormous support—but little scrutiny—from the United States.

Clinton beamed as Egypt's president, Hosni Mubarak, hosted a "summit of the peacemakers." American leaders have been smiling on the Egyptian government for a long time, with aid topping $2 billion a year since Mubarak came to power in 1981.

In return, Cairo has been a key ally in the Middle East—a role widely lauded by the U.S. press corps. Unfortunately, Egypt is also a nation of torture and political repression.

When asked about human rights, Egyptian officials like to talk about the anti-government Islamic radicals who kill innocent civilians. Egypt's embassy in Washington faxed us a statement that began by denouncing "extremists who falsely robe themselves in the garment of Islam."

America's leaders are quick to condemn the insurgents who have used murderous violence in Egypt during the past four years. Such condemnation is fully justified.

However, the White House doesn't seem concerned that police-state tactics and sham elections are central to the success of Egypt's ruling National Democratic Party. Last year [1995], opposition candidates encountered arrests and other harassment from police. The campaign culminated in November with flagrant vote-rigging.

"The elections took place as the government continued its crackdown on the Muslim Brotherhood—a fundamentalist group which was banned from the poll," Britain's *Daily Telegraph* reported. "Unlike militant Islamic groups which have attacked government targets, the group has always called for peaceful change."

The grim reality is that seeking peaceful change means grave dangers for Egyptians. Consider what Amnesty International concluded in its 1995 report on human rights in Egypt:

- "Dozens of lawyers and a number of journalists were arrested and detained as prisoners of conscience."

- "Torture of political detainees was systematic."

- "Thousands of suspected members or sympathizers of banned Islamic groups were detained under state-of-emergency legislation. Some were held without charge or trial; others, almost all civilians, received grossly unfair trials before military courts."

In November [1995], when a military court sentenced 54 dissidents to several years of prison with hard labor, Human Rights Watch denounced "expansion of the use of the military justice system to prosecute Egyptian civilians for the peaceful exercise of the right to freedom of association and expression."

Human Rights Watch stressed that "none of those sentenced were accused of offenses involving violence but were prosecuted solely for open, peaceful activities."

Much of the turmoil in Egypt is connected to the fact that acute poverty afflicts most of the country's 60 million people, while elites live in splendor. That gap keeps growing. A recent article in *Jane's Defense Weekly* describes "deep discontent among a population increasingly unrepresented, frustrated and poor."

The Feb. 28 [1996] article points out: "Rather than widening political participation to isolate the extremists and broaden the government's support base, Mubarak is imposing increasingly harsh measures that can only bolster sympathy for the Islamic militants."

The U.S. State Department has publicly noted some of Egypt's transgressions. However, as Human Rights Watch official Christopher George told us, "the problem is, it doesn't translate into policy." In other words, Washington is so cozy with Cairo that there's little pressure on Egypt to improve.

That's where our news media come in—or should. Independent reporting could shed harsh light on Egypt. Instead, journalists routinely seem to take their cues from the White House.

Yet, coverage occasionally provides valuable clarity. Reporting that Mubarak "presides over Egypt with a degree of power approaching monarchy," a June 30 [1995] *Los Angeles Times* dispatch observed: "While Egypt describes itself as a democracy, in truth it is a near one-party state." Mubarak's party "maintains a firm grip on the People's Assembly, the mass media, the military and the internal security apparatus."

Such candid stories are few and far between. To make matters worse, American journalists tend to shrug off the extreme risks faced by their Egyptian colleagues. One of Egypt's new laws is now resulting in lengthy prison sentences for Egyptian journalists who offend authorities.

The law forbids "false, deliberate or sensationalist reports aimed at disturbing public security, disdaining its national institutions or harming the country's economy"—just about any journalism that the Egyptian hierarchy doesn't like.

American media outlets are capable of reporting on human-rights violations in excruciating detail. But, as long as the Cairo government is popular among Washington policymakers, the chances are slim that we'll see much tough journalism about what's happening in Egypt.

March 13, 1996

As Lebanon Suffers,
Israel Can Count on U.S. Media Tilt

When bombs kill children and other civilians, outrage is a fitting response. Several weeks ago, condemnation was widespread after terrorist attacks on Israeli buses caused horrible carnage. But, more recently, with bombs taking innocent lives in Lebanon, the response from the United States has been quite different.

In the world according to U.S. media, the high moral ground in the Middle East belongs to Israel's government—even when it slaughters Lebanese civilians as a matter of policy. In news coverage, Israeli casualties are apt to have names, faces and bereaved relatives, while Arab victims are likely to be fleeting images: nameless, faceless, distant.

Yet, media spin cannot change realities on the ground. In mid-April [1996], with Israeli aircraft firing high-tech missiles at densely populated areas of Lebanon, the most deadly terrorist in the region was the prime minister of Israel.

Shimon Peres is the latest in a long line of Israeli leaders who have depended on plenty of cold cash from the U.S. government—a billion dollars every few months—and equally cold double-standards from American reporters and pundits.

Israel's most crucial allies include the mass media of the United States. Together with top officials in Washington, news outlets keep reinforcing the assumption that the Israeli government can do little wrong.

In the process, media treatment of Israel's relations with Lebanon has long been distorted. Ever since March 1978— when a U.N. Security Council resolution demanded unconditional withdrawal of Israeli troops from southern Lebanon—the U.S. media have made little note of the international illegality of Israel's occupation.

That occupation gained acceptance via the U.S. press, in part because of frequent use of an Orwellian phrase—"security zone"—to describe the several hundred square kilometers of Lebanese territory that Israel grabbed 18 years ago. During the current crisis, American journalism is still inclined to parrot the Israeli doublespeak.

So, on April 15 [1996], the front page of *USA Today* reported that "Israel moved to double the security zone it controls in Lebanon." The next day, on National Public Radio's *Morning Edition*, an NPR reporter was flatly referring to Israel's "security zone"—without even hinting that the phrase was invented to garner legitimacy for an illegitimate occupation.

We're told that Israel has a right to defend its northern border against rocket attacks by the Hezbollah militia based in Lebanon. Typically, certain key facts go unmentioned:

- Israel has been engaged in military assaults on southern Lebanon since the early 1970s, often bombing civilian targets.

- Israel's 1982 invasion of Lebanon resulted in the deaths of perhaps as many as 20,000 people, mostly civilians.

- In July 1993, seven days of Israeli air strikes killed or wounded hundreds of Lebanese noncombatants.

- Israeli soldiers have remained in southern Lebanon despite formal requests for withdrawal made repeatedly by the United Nations and Lebanon's government.

- Working in collaboration with the Israeli army inside the so-called "security zone," the mercenary South Lebanon Army continues to use systematic torture and abuse of prisoners.

For Americans, the ongoing bloodshed in Lebanon is more than a faraway tragedy. Our tax dollars have financed Israel's new blitzkrieg, complete with unconscionable bombardment of Beirut's civilian infrastructure. And, as the White House has made clear, the U.S. government provided a green light for Israel to proceed with airborne attacks.

Given their economic and political dependence on Washington, the leaders of Israel have a huge stake in American

Faliha Haidari, Lebanese refugee, stands with her children in front of U.N. shelter in southern Lebanon destroyed by Israeli shelling that killed over 75 people. The attack occurred two days after this column was written.

public opinion. Vigorous debate about Israeli policies, however, is not on the media agenda.

In the United States, on the rare occasions when TV networks present commentators who find fault with Israel, they're usually Arab diplomats rather than U.S. citizens. Yet, many Americans—including quite a few Jews—have come to oppose Israeli policies.

For decades, strong critics of Israel have encountered charges of anti-Semitism. The constant threat of the accusation has a chilling effect on debate. But, sadly, there's not much to chill. Even when the lives of children hang in the balance, the U.S. media debate about Israel seems to end before it begins.

April 17, 1996

News Coverage of Russian Election: Too Simple

Long ago, Winston Churchill described Russia as "a riddle wrapped in a mystery inside an enigma." But present-day news coverage of the Russian election has little room for complexity. The main story line resembles a wrestling match on American television.

In one corner, wearing star-spangled trunks, Boris Yeltsin!

In the other corner, wearing faded red trunks, Gennadi Zyuganov!

The June 17 [1996] issue of *Time* magazine summed up the contest as "an election that pits an imperfect and often corrupt capitalism against nostalgia for Stalinist glories." Most U.S. media accounts share a similar outlook.

Much is missing from such stories. For example:

- *Russian public health is a huge catastrophe.*

    Since 1989, life expectancy for Russian males has plummeted from 65 to 58. New cases of diphtheria now occur at a yearly rate of 35,000. Today, according to Russia's official statistics, only 40 percent of babies are born healthy.

    "Any one of these numbers is a horror," says Georgetown University professor Murray Feshbach, a longtime specialist in Russian health. The CBS program *60 Minutes* aired a notable May 19 [1996] report on Russia's ongoing health disaster. But several weeks later, Feshbach observes, American journalists still generally treat it as a "non-issue."

- *During the last few years, touted "reforms" have done enormous harm.*

    The usual media spin portrays Russia as a land in dire need of more "market reforms." Yet, they've already led to the ravaging of medical care, high unemployment and a plunge into poverty for 30 percent of the population.

So-called reforms have shredded much of the Russian safety net. Many people feel desperate—and yearn to regain a sense of security. But the American press is apt to ignore or belittle their desperation. In mid-June, a *Time* article simply depicted Zyuganov's constituency as "pensioners and those left out of the new, rambunctious Russian society."

- *Washington's "free market" agenda for Russia is designed to serve corporate interests, from oil to chickens to TV schlock.*

Atlantic Richfield recently announced plans to invest $3 billion in Russia and elsewhere in the former Soviet Union. Another oil company, Mobil, is financing a 900-mile pipeline to the Russian port at Novorossiysk.

Since 1992, U.S. chicken exports to Russia have gone from near zero to well over $500 million a year. Russia is now the biggest overseas market for the Tyson Foods poultry firm, owned by Don Tyson, an early supporter of Bill Clinton's 1992 presidential bid. Tyson also contributes frequently to congressional campaigns.

Starting this fall, Russians will be able to eat chicken while watching *Dallas*—dubbed in Russian—on television five nights a week. Handling ad sales for 357 episodes, media brokers boast that the show "will rivet viewers throughout Russia."

- *In Russia for the past half-decade, corruption and privatization have gone hand in hand.*

The rush to privatize has made a few Russians fabulously wealthy. The corruption is extreme. Formerly state-owned natural resources worth tens of billions of dollars—such as vast reserves of oil, natural gas and metals—now belong to a coterie of well-connected Russian bankers, swindlers and industrialists.

Overall, much of the reporting we get from Russia is skewed by assumptions at U.S. news organizations. "From what I've seen, they still have that Cold War chip on their shoulder," says the Moscow correspondent for Canadian Press service, Fred Weir, who has lived in Russia for 10 years. "They tend to see everything in terms of the struggle between good democrats and nasty commies."

When we reached him in Moscow a few days ago, Weir said he was "appalled at the way the Western media have accepted, with only mild hand-wringing, the total, Soviet-like domination of the Russian media by the Yeltsin administration." Ironically, Yeltsin's media control is "excused, even defended, by many Western journalists"—whose attitudes are "doing more to undermine freedom of the press in Russia than anything Zyuganov would be likely to do if he became president."

While disdaining Zyuganov as a wooden Communist ideologue, many U.S. reporters and pundits bring an equally rigid ideology to their coverage of Russia. When journalists so often equate democratic change with "economic reforms" favored by Western banks and the U.S. government, independent thinking is in short supply.

June 12, 1996

Part XV
Media-Speak

Judging from the proliferation of feel-good buzz-words and high-tech hype, an awesome march of progress will overcome current social and political problems. But bleak realities lurk beneath the surface of ubiquitous media-speak.

The Adventures of "Reform" in Medialand

"When I use a word," Humpty Dumpty declared, "it means just what I choose it to mean—neither more nor less."

But Alice was not convinced. "The question is," she replied, "whether you can make words mean so many different things."

For decades, the word "reform" had a clear meaning. Measures to uproot corruption, or end discrimination, or alleviate poverty, or advance the rights of working people—such programs were known as reforms.

No more. The 1990s have seen a drastic shift—to the point that news media now routinely use "reform" as the opposite of its original meaning.

"Reform" is one of the most popular words of contemporary journalism. Last year [1995], a half-dozen big newspapers —the *New York Times*, the *Washington Post*, the *Los Angeles Times*, the *Chicago Tribune*, *USA Today* and the *Boston Globe*—used it a total of 16,474 times.

These days, a lot of media attention is devoted to "reform" efforts in foreign countries. But not much of the coverage examines the negative consequences.

A recent front-page *New York Times* article began: "Distancing himself from the economic reforms that are the hallmark of his presidency, President Boris N. Yeltsin today accepted the resignation of Anatoly B. Chubais, a pillar of economic reform." The next paragraph described Chubais as "a beacon of free-market reform to the West." And a large-print pull-quote proclaimed: "A beacon of free-market reform becomes a scapegoat."

Such loaded news reports have a way of echoing the themes of editorials. A week earlier, in the same newspaper, an editorial essay used some form of the word "reform" 17 times in a nine-paragraph plea for vigorous Western aid to "reformers in the old Soviet Union." The essay lauded "the rudiments of market reform"—defined as Russian government steps to "decontrol prices, privatize state-owned enterprises and control its budget deficit."

If only things were so simple.

In Russia, those measures led to skyrocketing food prices and mass unemployment, while millions of elderly pensioners became destitute. Yet, as January [1996] ended, a spate of press commentaries in the United States were calling for the Clinton administration to exert more pressure on Yeltsin to stay the "reform" course.

Too often, American journalists take their cues from U.S. officials chanting "reform" buzzwords. Secretary of State Warren Christopher was in typical form a couple of weeks ago when he commented on Russian affairs: "We're very strongly supportive of the reformers who want to continue the reform."

Frequently, media accounts depict the opponents of "reform" as people trying to hold up progress by clinging to a bygone era. So, in Western Europe, according to a *Los Angeles Times* dispatch, reform-minded governments are "moving to cut public spending, privatize state companies and deregulate industries. And those reforms face stiff resistance from Europeans wedded to worker perks and generous social-welfare benefits."

Under a Rio de Janeiro dateline, the *Chicago Tribune* recently reported glad tidings—thanks to "market reforms"—from Latin America: "Economists say...the outlook for 1996 is improving. The best news, they say, is that open-market reforms, crafted over more than a decade, survived...despite sometimes intense pressure to dismantle them."

Translation: Economists selected by the *Chicago Tribune* are in favor of policies that have been exacerbating widespread poverty among South American people, whose protests must be rebuffed.

Since the 1980s, "structural adjustment programs"—championed by the International Monetary Fund and the World Bank —have taken hold in scores of countries. Most U.S. media outlets give short shrift to the harsh effects.

North American reporters and pundits are apt to praise "market reforms" when a foreign government halts food subsidies and removes barriers to food imports—while the affected population deals with climbing prices and a sharp rise in malnutrition.

Meanwhile, on the domestic front, damage to our social safety net is frequently abetted by the rhetoric of "reform."

Few eyebrows go up when journalists inform us of proposals for Medicare and Medicaid "reforms"—in other words, reductions in what the federal government would otherwise spend on health care for America's seniors.

As 1996 got underway, a *Boston Globe* news article mentioned that a "sweeping reform package" had taken effect in Massachusetts, banning "additional cash payments to mothers on welfare who have more children." To call such measures "reform" is to provide a favorable gloss for depriving children of basic assistance.

True, "reform" is just a word. But, used often and widely enough, a word can have plenty of influence. As George Orwell observed, normal language "becomes ugly and inaccurate because our thoughts are foolish, but the slovenliness of our language makes it easier for us to have foolish thoughts."

Just ask Humpty Dumpty.

January 31, 1996

TV News Diet:
From Sound Bites to "Sound Nibbles"

Soon after Richard Nixon moved into the White House, a new book—titled *The Selling of the President, 1968*—caused an uproar. On the cover was the jolting image of a cigarette pack with Nixon's picture on it.

Back then, the idea of marketing a candidate like a pack of cigarettes seemed scandalous. Today, we don't give it a second thought: We just assume that high-powered ad campaigns will pitch candidates much like any other "product."

In contrast to the TV commercials bought by politicians, news on the tube is supposed to be informative. Yet, in the real world, TV news coverage is more superficial than ever.

During the 1968 presidential race, when Nixon squared off against Hubert Humphrey, the average length of one of their sound bites on network TV news was 43 seconds. By 1988, when George Bush and Michael Dukakis ran for president, the average length had dropped to *nine* seconds.

These days, the notion of sound bites is obsolete. A more fitting term for televised snippets of political rhetoric would be "sound nibbles." Which should raise a key question: What, of substance, can be said in nine seconds?

About all that a politician—or anyone—can hope to do in nine seconds is reinforce existing assumptions. Most politicians try to do that with a vengeance, pushing buttons that are already well established.

Although the media bias in favor of brevity may seem even-handed, some candidates benefit from TV news reporting that gives short shrift to what they say.

For one thing, modern newscasts leave a vacuum for paid commercials to fill. The TV ad blitz by Steve Forbes was the main reason that he could begin this year as a serious presidential contender.

What's more, if candidates are heard for only a few moments on the evening news, the advantage goes to the ones who appeal to pre-existing prejudices. Sound nibbles can come off as snappy and cogent if they reinforce what people have heard many times before—and are already inclined to believe.

But, what if someone running for office has a perspective rarely heard in mass media? That outlook will probably require some explaining—more than just a few seconds—in order to make much sense.

Granted, many politicians do very well when they're heard in a jiffy. Some even *need* an extremely short time-limit to sound good. Take Ross Perot, for instance. He can be a real nine-second wonder. But, if you listen to his efforts to expound for much longer than that, you might start to notice that he has a lot of trouble connecting the mental dots. Brief aphorisms can be charming— but, strung end to end, they're apt to wear thin.

When television provides a few uninterrupted sentences from politicians, says media scholar Daniel Hallin, "you get some sense of how they think." Hallin, who studies TV news, has observed that a half-minute excerpt from a politician "affords the viewer a chance to perceive something of the person's character and to assess the merits of his or her argument in a way no 10-second sound bite can."

Even in prolonged settings, many political pros are all too glib. The consummate French politician Charles de Gaulle once began a press conference by telling reporters: "Gentlemen, I am ready for the questions to my answers."

It's true that listening to a politician at length is ordinarily no treat. But, in the era of the sound nibble, we're becoming accustomed to a meager diet that doesn't allow us to digest much of anything.

When politicians can get away with talking like bumper stickers, we get used to listening for slogans—and not much else. Sadly, our attention span tends to parallel our thinking span. What passes for TV journalism encourages us to mistake buzz-words for ideas.

As the 1996 campaign lurches forward, many Americans might be able to identify with a comment made long ago by Groucho Marx: "I find television very educational," he said. "Every time someone switches it on, I go into another room and read a good book."

March 27, 1996

Cyberspace Hype
Feeds Big Illusions

Midway through 1996, no media image is more appealing —or more misleading—than the wondrous realm known as cyberspace.

By now, most print and broadcast outlets are deeply involved in cyberhype. News reports keep track of cybercompetition. Feature stories extol the savvy moves of cyberinvestors. Commentators hail our cyberfuture. And, as you may have already noticed, writers strain to invent new "cyber" words.

It's pleasant to believe that the Internet will provide a free flow of information and opinion. The rhetoric makes plenty of egalitarian claims—but the emerging reality is something else.

"The Internet is in full transition from a participatory interactive communications network to a broadcast medium dominated by electronic commerce," observes Frank Beacham, a journalist who monitors technology. Viewed from corporate boardrooms, the ideal Internet users will be passive consumers.

Smart money is betting that the most heavily visited sites on the World Wide Web will be the ones with deep pockets behind them. Lots of publicity and multimedia leverage will be crucial to steer a mass audience to particular spots on the vast Internet.

Perhaps no company is better positioned to do such steering than Microsoft. At the end of 1995, Microsoft announced plans to redirect its on-line strategies to the Internet, where the powerful firm is now implementing a financial battle plan based on advertising. As *Wired* magazine notes, Microsoft will "act like a broadcaster" in cyberspace. And when it comes to content, the resemblance to network television is striking.

Microsoft owner Bill Gates has chosen to team up his company with a news organization (NBC) led by Tom Brokaw, and a huge cable conglomerate (TCI) run by a Rush Limbaugh fan named John Malone. The thread that connects them all is the bottom line.

Such alliances promise to be enormously profitable for Microsoft. Gates may be at the cutting edge of cyberspace technology and ultramodern marketing. But his guiding principle —greed—is as old as the hills.

The way things are going, Beacham warns, the Internet will undergo a profound shift—"from being a participatory medium that serves the interest of the public to being a broadcast medium, where corporations deliver consumer-oriented information. Interactivity would be reduced to little more than sales transactions and e-mail."

With gee-whiz enthusiasm permeating so much media discussion of cyberspace, we tend to think of the Internet as a dramatic departure from the past. But this is hardly the first time that high-tech advances have been confused with grassroots democratic empowerment.

Fifteen years ago, as cable television arrived with great fanfare, the futurist Alvin Toffler discerned "a truly new era—the age of the de-massified media." Just around the corner was cable-wired democracy. "Instead of masses of people all receiving the same messages, smaller de-massified groups receive and send large amounts of their own imagery to one another."

Consider Toffler's paean to cable TV technology the next time you're flipping through the 57 channels—and, in the words of Bruce Springsteen, nothing's on.

It's easy to be mesmerized by a techno-fix that seems to offer a way of cutting through knotty social problems. To substitute for figuring out how to create systems of communication that are genuinely democratic, believers in the techno-fix assume that a brilliant new technology can dissolve the bottlenecks.

It never works. From radio to television to modem, each new gizmo has arrived with inspiring potential—undermined by extreme disparities in people's access to economic resources and political clout. Now, billionaire Bill Gates and his collaborators are smiling as they pour big investments into the Internet and tie those projects to other mass-media endeavors.

The middle of July [1996] brings the launch of MSNBC, a 24-hour news channel on cable television that's a joint venture of Microsoft and NBC (owned by General Electric). Many of the channel's programs will promote "interactive companion activities on the Internet." Rather than getting away from the centralized power of a network like NBC, such cyberspace "synergies" only amplify it.

"Microsoft's extensive reach into the interactive media business could well make it the world's first 21st-century media company," industry analyst Denise Caruso writes in *Wired*. Not a comforting thought.

June 26, 1996

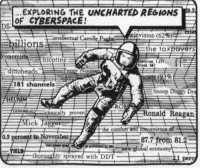

Part XVI
Fun and Games and Prizes

Congratulations on making it through this chronicle of media crimes and misdemeanors. Your reward: fun and games and prizes. Maybe you can laugh to keep from crying.

And Now It's Time for...
"Media Jeopardy!"

Thanks for joining us on "Media Jeopardy!"

A reminder of the rules: First, listen carefully to the answer. Then, try to come up with the correct question.

OK, let's get started. The first category is "Racial Pasts of Leading Pundits."

- Some of his fellow journalists are angry that he lied when he denied being "Anonymous." But he has continued to escape criticism from colleagues for writing *Newsweek* columns that stereotype inner-city blacks as dishonest.

  Who is Joe Klein?

- Today, many consider him to be the most influential commentator in America, and he enjoys a reputation for enlightened erudition—but few are aware that he was a speechwriter for Jesse Helms during the early 1970s.

  Who is George Will?

- In 1957, he wrote that Southern whites should prevail politically even when outnumbered by blacks in a local area. "The white community is so entitled because, for the time being, it is the advanced race," he declared—adding that "it is more important for any community, anywhere in the world, to affirm and live by civilized standards, than to bow to the demands of the numerical majority."

  Who is William F. Buckley?

Our second category is "The Liberal Media."

- This key Republican strategist and prominent TV pundit came clean recently when he said: "I admit it, the liberal media were never that powerful, and the whole thing was often used as an excuse by conservatives for conservative failures."

  Who is William Kristol?

- "The truth is, I've gotten fairer, more comprehensive coverage of my ideas than I ever imagined I would receive," this pundit-turned-presidential-candidate stated in March [1996]. He conceded: "I've gotten balanced coverage and broad coverage—all we could have asked.... For heaven sakes, we kid about the liberal media, but every Republican on Earth does that."

  Who is Patrick Buchanan?

- For years, he was cited as the left-wing voice among *New York Times* pundits. Yet, this syndicated columnist describes himself as "a pro-capitalist, middle-of-the-road, tepid centrist."

  Who is Anthony Lewis?

- Although he represented "the left" for six years on CNN's *Crossfire* program, this pundit identified himself as "a wishy-washy moderate."

  Who is Michael Kinsley?

Now, we move on to "Tube Politics."

- He served as media adviser for George Bush's successful and sleazy 1988 presidential campaign. Today, he has a different job title—"chairman of Fox News," owned by Rupert Murdoch.

  Who is Roger Ailes?

- The moderator of the network program *Fox News Sunday* is hardly neutral; he's been a frequent substitute radio-host for Rush Limbaugh and was chief speechwriter for President Bush.

Who is Tony Snow?

Now, it's on to "Great Moments in Punditry."

- In an editorial on June 29, 1981, this newspaper called for "complete deregulation" of the nation's savings and loan industry. Urging policy changes that ended up costing tax-payers hundreds of billions of dollars for the S&L bailout, the paper proclaimed: "The beauty of these solutions is that they're cheap."

What is the *Wall Street Journal*?

- On CNN's *The Capital Gang*, two days after the Iraqi invasion of Kuwait, he explained that U.S. military intervention was out of the question: "We're not going to send troops in there. C'mon, there's no chance of that."

Who is Robert Novak?

We're moving into Media Double Jeopardy with our next category, "Public Shmublic."

- This government agency is supposed to protect the public interest, but it persists in letting mega-media owners do just about whatever they want with the nation's airwaves.

What is the Federal Communications Comission?

- Executives at this "noncommercial" network have agreed to repeatedly broadcast the slogan of a hard-liquor brand in exchange for big contributions.

What is National Public Radio?

Fun and Games and Prizes

And now, we're in Final Media Jeopardy...

- This person has the most crucial role in evaluating the content of news media.

Who is reading these words?

July 24, 1996

Announcing
The P.U.-Litzer Prizes for 1995

It is time for us to announce the winners of the P.U.-litzer Prize for 1995.

Competition was intense for the fourth annual P.U.-litzers, which recognize some of the stinkiest media performances of the past year.

And now, the envelopes please.

UN-AMERICAN JOURNALISM PRIZE—Publisher Ted Owen, *San Diego Business Journal*

According to his staff, publisher Ted Owen banned photos of individuals of certain ethnic backgrounds (including Vietnamese, Iraqis and Iranians) from prominent spots in his weekly business journal on the grounds that such visible coverage was "un-American." Asked about the ban by a local daily, Owen commented: "It is not a public debate how I run the newspaper." But after protests from area businesses, Owen renounced any photo-apartheid policy.

PENTAGON PUNDIT AWARD—Mark Shields, Steve Roberts, et al.

This year, leading pundits Mark Shields, Steve Roberts, Gloria Borger, Haynes Johnson and Hedrick Smith received paychecks directly from Lockheed Martin—the country's top military contractor—to appear as regular panelists on a radio talk show in Washington. Lockheed Martin sees value in funding influential pundits across the media's narrow political spectrum, including TV liberals like Shields. Meanwhile, media "debates" about budget-balancing concentrate on cuts aimed at seniors and the poor, but not the Pentagon.

RELATIVELY TORTURED PROSE PRIZE—Reporter Nicholas Kristof, the *New York Times*

Writing of brutally repressive regimes on Dec. 4, Kristof observed: "While a relatively small number of South Koreans were tortured to death under Mr. Chun and Mr. Roh, the great majority of people gained during their rule."

"THEM, NOT ME" PRIZE—Editor-in-Chief Mort Zuckerman, *U.S. News & World Report*

Mort Zuckerman's magazine featured an Oct. 2 cover story titled "Tax Exempt!: You pay Uncle Sam. How come thousands of American corporations do not?" The article focused on non-profit corporations that don't pay taxes; it didn't mention that Zuckerman, the multimillionaire realtor who owns *U.S. News & World Report*, failed to pay any federal income taxes between 1981 and 1986.

FREQUENT FLYERS AWARD—*Time* magazine

Time, the nation's biggest newsweekly, spent $3 million to fly heads of corporations around the world for nine days this fall. *Time*'s top managers and editors escorted several dozen executives from blue-chip firms (such as General Motors, Lockheed Martin, Rockwell and Philip Morris) to India, Hong Kong, Vietnam, Russia and Cuba for private briefings with foreign heads of state. Will *Time*'s reporters be eager to scrutinize the firms their bosses have wined and dined across the globe?

ALL HAIL WALL STREET AWARD—*Christian Science Monitor*

Many news outlets rejoiced when the Dow Jones average topped 5,000, but a front-page *Christian Science Monitor* article on the day before Thanksgiving won first prize for sheer propaganda. Headlined "Wall St. Enriches Main St.," the article asserted that Wall Street's bull market has "helped millions of people, whether they have a stake in the market or just read about it." The celebratory article didn't mention the links between booming stock prices and corporate profits on one hand

and the downturn of income for American workers on the other. As the Economic Policy Institute concluded in a recent study, "Business profits have been fueled by stagnant or falling wages."

(DIS)HONEST TO GOD AWARD—Rush Limbaugh

In a June 12 radio oration, Rush Limbaugh accused the "liberal media" of refusing to mention that Capt. Scott O'Grady, the U.S. pilot shot down and rescued in Bosnia, had credited God. "I haven't found one printed reference to him thanking God." Limbaugh's "facts" were wrong (as usual); major dailies had repeatedly and prominently quoted O'Grady's references to God. "Pilot, Back at Base, Thanks God and His Rescue Crews," said a June 10 *New York Times* headline over a story that quoted O'Grady in paragraph two: "The first thing I want to do is thank God."

CORRECTION OF THE YEAR—*The New Yorker*

In an editor's note, *The New Yorker* magazine explained that conservative leader William Bennett had criticized presidential candidate Patrick Buchanan's politics as "a real us-and-them kind of thing"—not, as the magazine had previously reported, "a real S&M kind of thing."

"WAR IS PEACE" PRIZE—*Business Week* and Paul Craig Roberts

Commenting on Chile's 17-year military dictatorship that ended in 1990, *Business Week* writer Paul Craig Roberts lauded the regime for "restoring stability" and creating "a vast capital market." As for the Chilean government's murder of thousands of political dissidents during those years, Roberts credited the dictatorship with "suppressing...terror."

LIBERAL IDIOCY AWARD—Pundit Christopher Matthews

Discussing the federal minimum wage on *The McLaughlin Group*, liberal syndicated columnist Christopher Matthews told television viewers: "The big fight in this country is between the people who don't work on welfare and the people who do work."

LAMEST EXCUSE AWARD—Newspaper Association of America

Last summer, when a survey found that only 19 percent of the sources cited on newspaper front pages were women, Newspaper Association of America spokesperson Paul Luthringer tried to explain it this way: "The fact that women are quoted less than men has nothing to do with the state of journalism, but has more to do with who—male or female—is the first to return a reporter's phone call."

Unfortunately, space does not allow mention of the many runners-up for this year's P.U.-litzers. In the world of journalism, their lofty achievements had profound effects.

December 20, 1995

And Now,
The P.U.-Litzer Prizes for 1996

It's time now to reveal the winners of the P.U.-litzer Prizes for 1996.

This annual award recognizes some of America's most foul media achievements. Every year, for the past half-decade, we have pored through hundreds of submissions. In 1996, we've found many deserving entries. But only a few journalists can win a P.U.-litzer.

DEFAMING THE INFIDELS AWARD—Mort Zuckerman, owner and editor-in-chief, *U.S. News & World Report*

The head of *U.S. News & World Report* has excelled at casting aspersions on the Islamic faith. But Zuckerman reached a new low in his June 10 column, declaring that rhetoric by Palestinian leader Yasir Arafat "echoes the doctrine of the prophet Muhammad of making treaties with enemies while he is weak, violating them when he is strong." Offended Muslims pointed out to the magazine that the Koran requires the faithful to keep their pledges.

JUMPING THE GUN PRIZE —Clyde Haberman of the *New York Times*

With scant information on what caused the deadly TWA explosion near Long Island last summer, Haberman wrote a July 19 *Times* news article that began: "This may seem to be jumping the gun, since so much is still not known about what brought down Trans World Airlines Flight 800. But it is probably time for Americans to accept terrorism as a fact of life requiring certain impositions, like personal searches in public places, to preserve communal safety." In other words, it's never too soon to jettison some liberties.

CHAMPION OF THE OVERDOG PRIZE—ABC TV reporter John Stossel

In a September speech to a group of conservative attorneys, Stossel—whose recent specials and *20/20* segments have targeted unions, consumer lawyers and government regulation —spoke of why he'd moved away from consumer reporting: "I got sick of it. I also now make so much money I just lost interest in saving a buck on a can of peas." Stossel, who now functions as ABC's televangelist for what he calls "the beauties of the free market," told his audience: "I certainly would encourage any of you who knows somebody who buys advertising on television to say, 'Please buy a couple of ads on those Stossel specials.'" Markets certainly are things of beauty.

TALK RADIO BOMBS-AWAY AWARD—John Dayl of KFYI, Phoenix

In July, on Arizona's second-biggest talk station, host Dayl offered these words about U.S. government employees targeted in terrorist bombings like Oklahoma City: "These people who work in those buildings are not innocent victims. If they work in the Federal Building, they're the very people that are typing the letters, that are making the phone calls, that are getting our land taken away from you, that are calling you up on Internal Revenue Service, that want to confiscate all of your guns. These are the same people who womp up charges against you. These are the very same people that are all involved, every one of them....These people are not innocent victims."

TALK RADIO FIRE-AWAY AWARD—Rollye James of KLBJ, Austin

Agreeing with a caller who praised the bumper sticker, "Where is Lee Harvey Oswald when you need him?," talk host James added that Vice President Al Gore would also have to be shot, "perhaps with the same bullet." Wishing for a magic bullet cost James her job at KLBJ. Ironically, the radio station is owned by the family of Lyndon B. Johnson.

REVOLVING DOOR PRIZE—Patrick Buchanan and CNN

Buchanan, who has revolved between media and politics several times already, may well run for president again in four years. No sooner had he conceded defeat at the '96 convention than he was on CNN being beseeched by Larry King about his plans to return to that network: "Will you come back to *Crossfire* in November?" When Buchanan demurred, King even relayed an on-air invitation from CNN president Tom Johnson: "It's official—he wants you back on *Crossfire*." Thanks to CNN, Buchanan can wage his never-ending presidential campaign nightly on national television.

DEATH BY CENSORSHIP PRIZE—CNN's Susan Rook

In November, on CNN's *Talkback Live* hosted by Susan Rook, a caller asked a panel that included comedian Al Franken about the invisibility in mainstream discourse of leftist intellectual Noam Chomsky—currently one of our country's most prolific writers and most requested lecturers.

FRANKEN: "Susan, we never answered the question about Noam Chomsky. Why do you think you don't see enough Noam Chomsky on CNN?"

ROOK: "Are you asking me?"

FRANKEN: "Yeah."

ROOK: "Isn't he dead?"

FRANKEN: "No, no he isn't."

ROOK: "I thought he was dead."

NUZZLE THE HAND THAT FEEDS AWARD—Richard Bernstein, *New York Times* book critic

In a largely negative review of *Up From Conservatism*, Michael Lind's recent book about why he quit the right-wing movement, Bernstein objected to the book's criticisms of some well-funded conservative scholars. Lind is "disagreeable," Bernstein wrote—"disagreeable especially in his dismissal of a group of distinguished thinkers as little more than the hirelings of an evil system.... For Mr. Lind, the conservatives are a dishonest bunch who decree doctrine irrespective of the evidence, misrepresenting things on the orders of their moneyed patrons." Two of the moneyed patrons lambasted by Lind's book are the Bradley Foundation and the Smith-Richardson Foundation. In his review, Bernstein neglected to mention that those two funders had financed Bernstein's research for his 1994 book attacking multiculturalism.

WINE-TO-VINEGAR PRIZE—Public TV station KQED, San Francisco

Top managers at KQED were so eager to produce a documentary about California winemaker Robert Mondavi that they arranged to get $50,000 in seed money from a Mondavi-funded center for the wine industry—and lined up $150,000 more from the same source if work on the documentary pleased the center. A public uproar forced cancellation of the project in mid-November. Although independence from commercial sponsors is supposed to be a key reason for public TV's existence, the station still insists there was nothing wrong with the scheme.

LET THEM WATCH ADS AWARD—Local TV News

Just two weeks before the November election, Rocky Mountain Media Watch conducted a same-day survey of 68 local TV newscasts across the country—and found very little news about state and local races. About half of the newscasts contained no such news. Sixty-one percent of the 173 election stories that aired on "local" news were about the national presidential race. Since most Americans say they get their news from TV, what they got primarily was political ads: There were nearly three times as many commercials about local and state races as news stories.

FLIPPING FOR BIG MACS AWARD—Thomas Friedman, *New York Times* columnist

In a pair of December columns (datelined from the McDonald's world headquarters in Oak Brook, Ill.), Friedman argued that the fast-food chain exemplifies the beneficent potential of a globalized economy. He hailed McDonald's for showing sensitivity to various cultures and "democratizing globalization so that people everywhere feel some stake in how it impacts their lives." For Friedman, apparently, relishing the corporatization of the planet is an acquired taste.

Space limits preclude honoring more contestants. But competition for the 1997 P.U.-litzer Prizes begins soon—on New Year's Day.

December 18, 1996

Time Capsule for News Media

Let's seal a time capsule that could convey something to future generations about America's news media in 1996.

A time capsule is a big responsibility. The people who might open this one, in 50 or 100 years, deserve facts that can provide some insight into the media of our era.

To leave a more favorable impression, let's skip the lowbrow stuff on television and radio—concentrating, instead, on sizable U.S. newspapers and wire services. With the help of a Nexis database search, from the first day of 1996 until mid-December, we can shed some light on the priorities of our higher-quality news outlets:

Journalists were clearly aware of homeless people, mentioned in 29,130 stories. And the word "poverty" cropped up in 34,851 articles. Amid huge gaps between rich and poor, certain ideas were routine in the press. "Free enterprise" was a familiar buzz phrase, appearing in 3,489 stories; even more common were "property rights" (6,802) and "free market" (9,345).

But other fiscal concepts were far less prominent in the same media outlets. "Labor rights" got a mere 440 mentions. "Economic justice" didn't do much better at 592. And as for "economic democracy"—well, that phrase turned up in only 38 stories.

News media of 1996 were receptive to war metaphors aimed at certain social problems. The term "war on drugs," for instance, was utilized in 3,510 different articles. However, enthusiasm for "war on poverty" lagged way behind at 685.

How about "war on racism"? Seven stories. "War on discrimination"? Two. And "war on injustice" was an ultimate loser: zero.

The epithet "politically correct"—widely used to disparage those who challenge inequality—remained quite popular, showing up in 5,143 separate media pieces. On the other hand, the adjective most commonly used to describe bias against females, "sexist," appeared much less often: 3,190 times. And although hatred of women continued to be a significant problem in American society, the word for it—"misogyny"—could be found just 389 times.

Meanwhile, fascination with computer technology was immense. "Internet" popped up in 169,886 stories. Compare that total to "safety net"—mentioned in a paltry 6,761 stories, even though 1996 turned out to be the year when Washington withdrew the federal safety net for poor children that had been in place for six decades.

"Welfare reform" was a hot media phrase, repeated in 22,013 news pieces about aid programs for the poor. But "corporate welfare"—a phrase referring to federal aid to dependent business firms costing taxpayers an estimated $125 billion per year—surfaced in only 2,351 media spots. And the rallying cry of "corporate welfare reform" was a forlorn non-starter with 17 appearances.

Moving to less weighty topics, at least the American press showed it wasn't too nationalistic to keep covering Britain's Princess Di, who drew notice in just over 5,000 stories. Domestic celebs also got plenty of ink. So, there were 2,604 articles that referred to America's odious shock-jock Howard Stern—while Howard Zinn, one of this nation's wisest historians, received 36 mentions.

The Spanish heartthrob Antonio Banderas came in at 1,972. Carolyn Bessette, who distinguished herself by marrying John F. Kennedy Jr. in October, quickly scored 963. ("She has what it takes to be a true style icon in the new millennium: a look that's both raunchy and regal," *Newsweek* reported in very big type.)

The Kennedy-Bessette marriage came several months after an auction of items from the Jacqueline Kennedy Onassis estate resulted in mega-publicity. "Going Once...Going Twice...Going Crazy!" exclaimed the cover of *Time*, which featured a picture of John-John's sister Caroline sucking on her mother's pearls in 1958. The phrase "Jackie's pearls" garnered 15 different mentions, and the auction at Sotheby's more than 1,200.

For journalists, however, it may be sobering to consider just how little media space was devoted to trailblazing predecessors who exemplified reportorial courage. The great foreign correspondent and press critic George Seldes died last year at the age of 104 after a brilliant career spanning many of the century's momentous events. Seldes got 25 mentions. The gutsy independent journalist I.F. Stone got 16. Famed muckrakers Lincoln Steffens and Ida Tarbell: 43 and 20 respectively.

Lisa Marie Presley: 861. Kato Kaelin: 1,145. Fergie: 1,653. Nike: 14,443. Native Americans and human rights: 293.

"Entrepreneur": 23,755. "Social justice worker": 2.

Snowboarding: 3,220. Comparable to "poor children": 3,179.

Well, time to seal this time capsule. When it's unearthed, what will people think of our news media?

December 11, 1996

Index

Index

B

Bagdikian, Ben, 108, 167
Baker, Chuck, 49-51, 106
Banderas, Antonio, 276
Banzer, Hugo, 230
Barger, Brian, 219
Bari, Judi, 119-120
Barsamian, David, 12
Beacham, Frank, 258-259
Beckel, Bob, 42, 44
Bellant, Russ, 61, 63
Bell South, 146
Bennett, William, 61, 65-68, 268
Bergman, Walter, 200
Berkowitz, Herb, 59-61
Bermudez, Enrique, 215
Bernstein, Carl, 222-223
Bernstein, Richard, 272-273
Bessette, Carolyn, 276
Bird, Kai, 187
Black Panther Party, 202-203
Blackstone Rangers, 202-203
Blair, Joseph, 230
Blandon, Oscar Danilo, 211-212, 215-218
Bliley, Thomas, Jr., 157
block grants, 150-153
Bob Dole (Cramer), 163
Bogdanich, Walt, 84
Boggs, Thomas, 8
Bohmer, Peter, 202
Bolivia, 230
Bonasia, Jay, 165
Borger, Gloria, 266
Bosnia, 268
Boston Globe, 195, 203, 252, 254
Bourgeois, Roy, 231-232
Boyd, Sean, 53
Braden, Tom, 42, 45
Bradley Foundation, 58, 273
Brady, Sarah, 51
Brady Bill (gun control), 49
The Brass Check (Sinclair), 1, 2
Braverman, Alan, 84
Break-ins, Death Threats and the FBI (Gelbspan), 203

Brewer, John, 47
Brinkley, David, 9-10, 185
Broder, James, 46
Brokaw, Tom, 17, 135, 172, 258
Brookings Institution, 175, 206
Brown, Jerry, 36
Browne, Harry, 174
Buchanan, Patrick, 26, 36-39, 41, 42-44, 45, 86, 201, 263, 268, 272
Buckley, William F., 46, 47, 70-71, 262
Bulletin of the Atomic Scientists, 191
Bush, George, 4, 98, 147, 255, 263-264
Bush administration, 41, 129, 162, 198
Business Week, 268

C

Cable News Network, *See* CNN
cable television, 4, 6, 70, 104, 135, 259-260
   See also television
Calero, Adolfo, 213
Callejas, Manuel Antonio, 230
Cameron, James, 1
campaign contributions, 4, 5, 146, 163, 169, 171-172, 174-176
   See also presidential campaigns
Canadian Press Service, 249
Cannistraro, Vincent, 213
The Capital Gang (CNN), 264
Capone, Al, 207
Carey, Pete, 216
Caribbean, 127-129, 182-184, 197, 230
   See also Latin America; *specific nations*
Carlson, Richard, 71
Carreño, Jose, 238
Carrigan, Ana, 233
Carter, Jimmy, 143-144, 226-228
Caruso, Denise, 260
Casey, William, 142
Castano, Fidel, 236
Cato Institute, 20
CBS, 147, 168, 198, 247
   See also specific programs
CBS Evening News, 104
CBS News, 55, 217

279

Index

Index

Index

Index

Corporate Wizards of Media Oz

Top Ten Owners

Time Warner	**TCI**
Disney	**Seagram**
Viacom	**Westinghouse**
News Corp/Murdoch	**Gannett**
Sony	**General Electric**

Credits

Cartoons by Matt Wuerker: Pages 13, 29, 60, 173, 176

Cartoons by Tom Tomorrow: Pages 43, 52, 159, 214, 255, 258

Photographs by Jennifer Warburg: Pages 37, 64, 67, 148, 164, 230

Photo on page 24 by Kathy Willens, AP/Wide World Photos

Cartoon on page 32 by Paul Conrad Copyright, 1995, *Los Angeles Times*. Reprinted by permission.

Cartoon on page 73 by Kirk Anderson, St. Paul, Minn.

Cartoon on page 79 by TOLES © 1995. Reprinted with permission of UNIVERSAL PRESS SYNDICATE. All rights reserved.

Photos on page 112: Jackson Hill, *We Do The Work*; Fred Solowey, *New Teamster, Solidarity*

Cartoon on page 152 by TOLES © 1995 *The Buffalo News*. Reprinted with permission of UNIVERSAL PRESS SYNDICATE. All rights reserved.

Cartoon on page 170 by Clay Butler, Capitola, Calif.

Photo on page 235 by Herney Patiño, *Colombia Hoy* and *Cambio 16*

Photo on page 243 by Ali Mohamed, AP/Wide World Photos

About the Authors

Norman Solomon and Jeff Cohen are the co-authors of two previous collections of columns, *Adventures in Medialand: Behind the News, Beyond the Pundits* and *Through the Media Looking Glass: Decoding Bias and Blather in the News.*

Norman Solomon writes a nationally syndicated column, "Media Beat," distributed to daily newspapers by Creators Syndicate and to weeklies by AlterNet. His book *False Hope: The Politics of Illusion in the Clinton Era* was published in 1994. He is author of *The Power of Babble* and co-author (with Martin A. Lee) of *Unreliable Sources: A Guide to Detecting Bias in News Media.* His commentary articles have appeared in the *New York Times, Washington Post, Miami Herald, International Herald Tribune* and many other newspapers. He has been a guest on C-SPAN, CNN's *Crossfire* and NPR's *Talk of the Nation.* Solomon is executive producer of the international radio program *Making Contact.* He lives in the San Francisco area with his wife Cheryl Higgins.

Jeff Cohen is the founder and executive director of FAIR (Fairness & Accuracy In Reporting), the media watch organization based in New York City. He works closely with activist groups across the country on media bias and censorship issues. He has appeared as a guest on national TV programs like *Larry King Live, Donahue* and *Today*—and has co-hosted CNN's *Crossfire.* He has written for many publications, including the *Los Angeles Times, Washington Post, Newsday, USA Today, Mother Jones* and *Rolling Stone.* Cohen is co-author of *The Way Things Aren't: Rush Limbaugh's Reign of Error.* He resides near Woodstock, New York, with his wife, Stephanie Kristal, and their daughters Sequoia and Cassidy.

The authors frequently lecture on college campuses. Norman Solomon can be reached by phone at (510) 273-9002, via e-mail at <mediabeat@igc.org> or by mail at P.O. Box 13193, Oakland, CA 94661. Jeff Cohen can be contacted c/o FAIR, 130 W. 25th St., New York, NY 10001; (212) 633-6700, fax (212) 727-7668.

FAIR produces the weekly radio show *Counterspin*, and the magazine *EXTRA!* To subscribe to *EXTRA!*, call 1-800-847-3993. FAIR's website is <www.fair.org/fair>.